Instant Weka How-to

Implement cutting-edge data mining aspects in Weka to your applications

Boštjan Kaluža

[PACKT]
PUBLISHING

BIRMINGHAM - MUMBAI

Instant Weka How-to

Copyright © 2013 Packt Publishing

All rights reserved. No part of this book may be reproduced, stored in a retrieval system, or transmitted in any form or by any means, without the prior written permission of the publisher, except in the case of brief quotations embedded in critical articles or reviews.

Every effort has been made in the preparation of this book to ensure the accuracy of the information presented. However, the information contained in this book is sold without warranty, either express or implied. Neither the author, nor Packt Publishing, and its dealers and distributors will be held liable for any damages caused or alleged to be caused directly or indirectly by this book.

Packt Publishing has endeavored to provide trademark information about all of the companies and products mentioned in this book by the appropriate use of capitals. However, Packt Publishing cannot guarantee the accuracy of this information.

First published: June 2013

Production Reference: 1170613

Published by Packt Publishing Ltd.
Livery Place
35 Livery Street
Birmingham B3 2PB, UK.

ISBN 978-1-78216-386-2

www.packtpub.com

Credits

Author
Boštjan Kaluža

Reviewer
Anutosh Ghosh

Acquisition Editor
Usha Iyer

Commissioning Editor
Poonam Jain

Technical Editors
Worrell Lewis
Dominic Pereira

Project Coordinator
Esha Thakker

Proofreader
Linda Morris

Production Coordinator
Prachali Bhiwandkar

Cover Work
Prachali Bhiwandkar

Cover Image
Conidon Miranda

About the Author

Boštjan Kaluža, PhD is a researcher in artificial intelligence and ubiquitous computing. Since October 2008, he has been working at Jozef Stefan Institute, Slovenia. His research focuses on the development of novel algorithms and approaches, with an emphasis on human behavior analysis from sensor data using machine learning and data mining techniques. Boštjan has extensive experience in Java and Python, and lectures Weka in the classroom. He spent a year as a visiting researcher at the University of Southern California, where he studied suspicious and anomalous agent behavior in the context of security applications. He has published over 40 journal articles and conference papers.

About the Reviewer

Anutosh Ghosh loves coding, but has worked extensively only in the world of PHP for over five and a half years now. He has good knowledge of Magento and has worked on the integration of Magento Web Services with SAP for more than two and a half years.

He is also trying his hand in Java, as well as anything technical as and when he gets time. However, he loves to poke his blunt nose in some forums and Stack Overflow, from time to time.

When bored, he gets some recreation by watching movies and listening to songs. He can even be found singing some regional songs.

> I would like to thank my family for all their support, especially my mother and my wife for their enthusiastic and selfless support; without them, I could not have made it this far.

www.PacktPub.com

Support files, eBooks, discount offers and more

You might want to visit www.PacktPub.com for support files and downloads related to your book.

Did you know that Packt offers eBook versions of every book published, with PDF and ePub files available? You can upgrade to the eBook version at www.PacktPub.com and as a print book customer, you are entitled to a discount on the eBook copy. Get in touch with us at service@packtpub.com for more details.

At www.PacktPub.com, you can also read a collection of free technical articles, sign up for a range of free newsletters and receive exclusive discounts and offers on Packt books and eBooks.

PACKTLIB

http://PacktLib.PacktPub.com

Do you need instant solutions to your IT questions? PacktLib is Packt's online digital book library. Here, you can access, read and search across Packt's entire library of books.

Why Subscribe?

- Fully searchable across every book published by Packt
- Copy and paste, print and bookmark content
- On demand and accessible via web browser

Free Access for Packt account holders

If you have an account with Packt at www.PacktPub.com, you can use this to access PacktLib today and view nine entirely free books. Simply use your login credentials for immediate access.

Table of Contents

Preface   1
Instant Weka How-to   7
    Starting with Java and Weka (Simple)   8
    Loading the data (Simple)   13
    Filtering attributes (Simple)   17
    Selecting attributes (Intermediate)   20
    Training a classifier (Simple)   25
    Building your own classifier (Advanced)   28
    Tree visualization (Intermediate)   33
    Testing and evaluating your models (Simple)   35
    Regression models (Simple)   40
    Association rules (Intermediate)   44
    Clustering (Simple)   47
    Reusing models (Intermediate)   52
    Data mining in direct marketing (Simple)   53
    Using Weka for stock value forecasting (Advanced)   57
    Recommendation system (Advanced)   60

Preface

Data mining and machine learning are topics in artificial intelligence that focus on pattern discovery, prediction, and forecasting based on properties of collected data, while Weka is a toolbox implementing a variety of methods dedicated to those tasks. This book is about programming Weka in Java through practical examples.

Instant Weka How-To shows you exactly how to include Weka's machinery in your Java application. This book starts by importing and preparing the data, and then moves to more serious topics, such as classification, regression, clustering, and evaluation. For those of you who are eager to dive deeper, this book shows you how to implement online learning or to create your own classifier. This book includes several application examples, such as house price prediction, stock value forecasting, decision making for direct marketing, and a movie recommendation system.

Data mining is a hot topic in the industry, and Weka is an essential toolbox for Java. This book shows you how to stay ahead of the pack by implementing cutting-edge data mining aspects, such as regression and classification, and then moving to more advanced applications of forecasting, decision making, and recommendation.

What this book covers

Starting with Java and Weka (Simple) guides you through the process of preparing the environment to start with Java and Weka coding. It explains how to test your Weka installation and shows you how to prepare the Eclipse environment.

Loading the data (Simple) explains how to load a dataset in Weka's attribute-relation file format (ARFF), typically used to store training and testing data. In addition, it demonstrates how to create a dataset on-the-fly and save the data to a file.

Filtering attributes (Simple) demonstrates how to remove attributes after the dataset is loaded into Weka using supervised filters, which can take into account class attributes, and unsupervised filters, which disregard class attributes.

Selecting attributes (Intermediate) will explain how to find attributes that are relevant for the classification tasks, and how to select an evaluator, as well as a searching method that applies the selected evaluator on the attributes.

Training a classifier (Simple) addresses the most exciting task in data mining. It demonstrates how to train various classifiers, as well as how to build an incremental classifier, which does not need to be retrained from scratch after a new instance is added.

Building your own classifier (Advanced) covers the most essential steps required to design a functional classifier.

Tree visualization (Intermediate) demonstrates how to visualize a J48 decision tree, which can be extremely helpful to understand the underlying patterns in the tree.

Testing and evaluating your models (Simple) explains how to estimate classifier performance, that is, how accurate the model is when making its classifications. This recipe shows you how to assess the performance using a variety of measures and different evaluation techniques, such as separated train and test dataset, and k-fold cross-validation.

Regression models (Simple) explains how to use models that predict a value of numerical class, in contrast to classification, which predicts the value of a nominal class. Given a set of attributes, the regression builds a model, usually an equation that is used to compute the predicted class value.

Association rules (Intermediate) explains how to find frequent patterns, associations, correlations, or causal structures among sets of items or objects in transaction databases, relational databases, and so on. It's often used to do market basket analysis, as done by big supermarket chains to decide what products are often bought together; these are then placed close to each other in the store to increase the chance of people picking them up on impulse.

Clustering (Simple) demonstrates how to use clustering, that is, how to automatically group examples in the dataset by a similarity measure.

Reusing models (Intermediate) shows how to build a model, to save it into a bytestream as a file for later use, and to restore it into the original object.

Data mining in direct marketing (Simple) explains how to implement decision making to guide direct marketing in a company. It uses data from a real-world business problem that contains information on customers of an insurance company. The goal is to predict which of the customers in the train set will buy a caravan insurance policy.

Using Weka for stock value forecasting (Advanced) demonstrates how to forecast the next day's closing price using daily high, low, opening, and closing data for Apple Computer stocks.

Recommendation system (Advanced) demonstrates how to implement a recommendation system to suggest "customers who bought this item also bought..." It shows an approach based on collaborative filtering to recommend movies to a user.

What you need for this book

To run and implement recipes explained in this book, you will need the Java Development Kit (JDK) and Weka installed on your computer. Optionally, you can also install the Eclipse integrated development environment. Java works on many operating systems, including Windows, Linux and OS X.

Who this book is for

This book primarily targets Java developers who want to integrate Weka's data mining capabilities into their projects. Computer science students, data scientists, artificial intelligence programmers, and statistical programmers would equally gain from this book and would learn all about the essential tasks required to implement a project. Experience with Weka concepts is assumed.

Conventions

In this book, you will find a number of styles of text that distinguish between different kinds of information. Here are some examples of these styles, and an explanation of their meaning.

Code words in text are shown as follows: "Import a basic regression model `weka.classifiers.functions.LinearRegression`."

A block of code is set as follows:

```
import java.io.BufferedReader;
import java.io.FileReader;

import weka.core.Instance;
import weka.core.Instances;
import weka.classifiers.functions.LinearRegression;
```

Any command-line input or output is written as follows:

```
$javac -classpath ".;C:\Program Files\Weka-3-6\weka.jar" Test.java
```

New terms and **important words** are shown in bold. Words that you see on the screen, in menus or dialog boxes for example, appear in the text like this: "Select **Java Build Path** from the left menu, and choose the **Libraries** tab."

> Warnings or important notes appear in a box like this.

> Tips and tricks appear like this.

Reader feedback

Feedback from our readers is always welcome. Let us know what you think about this book—what you liked or may have disliked. Reader feedback is important for us to develop titles that you really get the most out of.

To send us general feedback, simply send an e-mail to feedback@packtpub.com, and mention the book title via the subject of your message.

If there is a topic that you have expertise in and you are interested in either writing or contributing to a book, see our author guide on www.packtpub.com/authors.

Customer support

Now that you are the proud owner of a Packt book, we have a number of things to help you to get the most from your purchase.

Downloading the example code

You can download the example code files for all Packt books you have purchased from your account at http://www.packtpub.com. If you purchased this book elsewhere, you can visit http://www.packtpub.com/support and register to have the files e-mailed directly to you.

Errata

Although we have taken every care to ensure the accuracy of our content, mistakes do happen. If you find a mistake in one of our books—maybe a mistake in the text or the code—we would be grateful if you would report this to us. By doing so, you can save other readers from frustration and help us improve subsequent versions of this book. If you find any errata, please report them by visiting http://www.packtpub.com/support, selecting your book, clicking on the **errata submission form** link, and entering the details of your errata. Once your errata are verified, your submission will be accepted and the errata will be uploaded on our website, or added to any list of existing errata, under the Errata section of that title. Any existing errata can be viewed by selecting your title from http://www.packtpub.com/support.

Piracy

Piracy of copyright material on the Internet is an ongoing problem across all media. At Packt, we take the protection of our copyright and licenses very seriously. If you come across any illegal copies of our works, in any form, on the Internet, please provide us with the location address or website name immediately so that we can pursue a remedy.

Please contact us at copyright@packtpub.com with a link to the suspected pirated material.

We appreciate your help in protecting our authors, and our ability to bring you valuable content.

Questions

You can contact us at questions@packtpub.com if you are having a problem with any aspect of the book, and we will do our best to address it.

Instant Weka How-to

Welcome to *Instant Weka How-to*. Data mining and machine learning are topics in artificial intelligence that focus on pattern discovery, prediction, and forecasting based on the properties of collected data, while Weka is a toolbox implementing a variety of methods dedicated to those tasks. This book is about programming Weka in Java through practical examples.

If you are new to programming Weka, then this is probably the best place to start. This book has been written with a purpose to provide a gentle tutorial over basic programming tasks using the Weka API.

As Weka is implemented in Java, the book is in essence a guide through some basic Weka coding in this language. The book shows you exactly how to include Weka's machinery in your Java application by implementing cutting-edge data mining algorithms such as regression and classification, and then moving to more advanced applications of forecasting, decision making, and recommendation. Although relying on Java, those of you who have some knowledge of programming won't need to learn Java first: the tutorial should be simple enough to skip learning Java itself.

The book assumes you are familiar with basic machine-learning methods and Weka concepts. For an in-depth explanation of the methods implemented in Weka including theoretical background and formal analysis, I recommend the book *Data Mining: Practical Machine Learning Tools and Techniques* by *Witten*, *Frank*, and *Hall*, the original authors of the Weka toolbox. However, if you are already familiar with the concepts, then this book can serve you as a quick cheat sheet for the common tasks.

Starting with Java and Weka (Simple)

This recipe will take you through the process of preparing the environment to start with Java and Weka coding.

Getting ready

To start developing an application in Java you need a **Java Development Kit** (**JDK**) installed on your computer. If you are not sure, follow the instructions given next. Some versions of Weka are shipped with **Java Virtual Machine** (**JVM**), which allows you to run Weka, but not to compile the code, so make sure the JDK is installed.

For those of you who are new to Java, Java programs are compiled to bytecode instructions with extension .CLASS. JVM is a program that executes those Java bytecode files on a particular host operating system. To run Java programs, you need a **Java Runtime Environment** (**JRE**), which basically includes JVM and some other libraries required to execute Java. Development of Java application requires JDK, which is a collection of programming tools, for example, javac compiler, jdb debugger, javadoc documentation generator, and many others. Java topic is covered in more detail in *Java 7 New Features Cookbook, Richard M. Reese* and *Jesse L. Reese, Packt Publishing*.

How to do it...

Let's list the steps required to complete the task.

1. Go to the Weka website at http://www.cs.waikato.ac.nz/ml/weka/.

> **Downloading the example code**
> You can download the example code files for all Packt books you have purchased from your account at http://www.packtpub.com. If you purchased this book elsewhere, you can visit http://www.packtpub.com/support and register to have the files e-mailed directly to you.

2. Click on the download link to get a self-extracting executable without the Java VM (weka-3-6-9.exe; 22.7 megabytes). For the OS X operating system, there is a single download option (weka-3-6-9.dmg).

> # Downloading and installing Weka
>
> There are two primary versions of Weka: the stable version corresponding to the latest edition of the data mining book, which only receives bug fixes, and the development version, which receives new features and exhibits a package management system that makes it easy for the Weka community to add new functionality to Weka. For the bleeding edge, it is also possible to download nightly snapshots.
>
> - **Snapshots**
>
>   Every night a snapshot of the Subversion repository is taken, compiled and put together in ZIP files. For those who want to have the latest bugfixes, they can download these snapshots **here**.
>
> - **Stable book 3rd ed. version**
>
>   Weka 3.6 is the latest stable version of Weka, and the one described in the 3rd edition of the **data mining book**. This branch of Weka receives bug fixes only (for new features in Weka see the developer version). There are different options for downloading and installing it on your system:
>
>   - **Windows x86**
>
>   Click **here** to download a self-extracting executable that includes Java VM 1.7 (weka-3-6-9jre.exe; 52.1 MB)
>
>   Click **here** to download a self-extracting executable without the Java VM (weka-3-6-9.exe; 22.7 MB)
>
>   These executables will install Weka in your Program Menu. Download the second version if you already have Java 1.6 (or later) on your system.

3. Run the installer and follow the instructions.

4. Write a simple test program using a text editor such as Notepad (on Windows) or TextEdit (on OS X) and save it as `Test.java` as follows:

   ```
   import weka.core.*;

   public class Test{
     public static void main(String args[]){
       System.out.println("Weka loaded.");
     }
   }
   ```

   Java is case sensitive, so make sure to pay attention to the case type.

5. Open Command Prompt on Windows (⊞ + *R*, enter `cmd`, and press *Enter*) or Terminal on OS X (**Applications | Terminal**).

Instant Weka How-to

6. Navigate to the folder where you saved the `Test.java` source file and compile the code with the following class path parameter.

    ❏ For Windows:

    ```
    $javac -classpath ".;C:\Program Files (x86)\Weka-3-6\weka.jar" Test.java
    ```

    ❏ For OS X:

    ```
    $javac -classpath ".;/Applications/weka-3-6/weka.jar" Test.java
    ```

7. Run the code.

    ```
    $ java Test
    Weka loaded.
    ```

If you get this output, congratulations, you are ready to move on to the next recipes.

How it works...

Since the first three steps are self-explanatory, we will start with the explanation from step 4. After the Weka is installed, we want to make sure we are ready to move on. In a simple `Test.java` program, some of the Weka's objects are loaded, for example:

```
import weka.core.*;
```

The reason we import this is only to make sure Weka is loaded. Therefore, the rest of the code simply writes a message that will let you know the program has executed and successfully loaded Weka:

```
public class Test{
  public static void main(String args[]){
    System.out.println("Weka loaded.");
  }
}
```

To compile the code we need to specify where the compiler can find the Weka objects—they are stored in Weka's installation folder as the `weka.jar` package. We simply pass this path to the compiler with the class path parameter as follows:

```
$javac -classpath ".;C:\Program Files\Weka-3-6\weka.jar" Test.java
```

If there is an error such as:

```
Test.java:8: error: package weka.core does not exist
import weka.core.*;
                ^
1 error
```

Then, the `weka.jar` path in the class path parameter is probably not specified correctly. Make sure it points to the Weka installation folder.

Finally, run the code and you should be able to see the output.

```
$ java Test
Weka loaded.
```

If you see this output, it means Weka was successfully loaded and we are ready to move on.

There's more...

This section will first explain how to check if JDK is installed and then demonstrate how to start a project in the Eclipse framework.

Check if JDK is installed

First, check which version of Java is installed. Open the command/terminal window and type the following command:

```
$ java -version
java version "1.7.0"
Java(TM) SE Runtime Environment (build 1.7.0-b147)
```

To check if you have JDK, type the following command in the command/terminal window:

```
$ javac
```

If you get an error, such as:

```
javac: command not found
```

Or alternatively on Windows:

```
'javac' is not recognized as an internal or external command,
operable program or batch file.
```

Then, the JDK may not be installed or it may not be in your path. You can use your system's file search utilities to see if there is a `javac` or `javac.exe` executable installed. If it is, and it is a recent enough version (Java 1.6 or Java 1.7, for example), you should put the bin directory that contains `javac` in your system path. The Java runtime, `java.exe`, is often in the same bin directory. To add it to the system path, open Command Prompt (or Terminal in OS X), navigate to the `javac` directory, and type the following:

```
PATH=%PATH%;%CD%
```

Instant Weka How-to

If a JDK is not already on your system, you should download one. The JDK is available on the Oracle website but it requires your choice of platform to proceed. Be sure to select a JDK that matches not only your operating system but also your hardware system.

Working with Eclipse

Eclipse is a free and open source **Integrated Development Environment** (**IDE**); that is, an application that provides source code editor, compiler, debugger, and many other features. It significantly increases programmer productivity and simplifies many tasks. For more details read *Instant Eclipse Application Testing How-to, Anatoly Spektor, Packt Publishing*.

Eclipse can be downloaded from http://www.eclipse.org/downloads. If you are not sure which version is right for you, just pick Eclipse Classic and follow the installation wizard.

To start a new project using Weka, perform the following steps:

1. Create a new Java project by going to **File** | **New** | **Java Project** and enter a project name, for example, MyWekaApp.

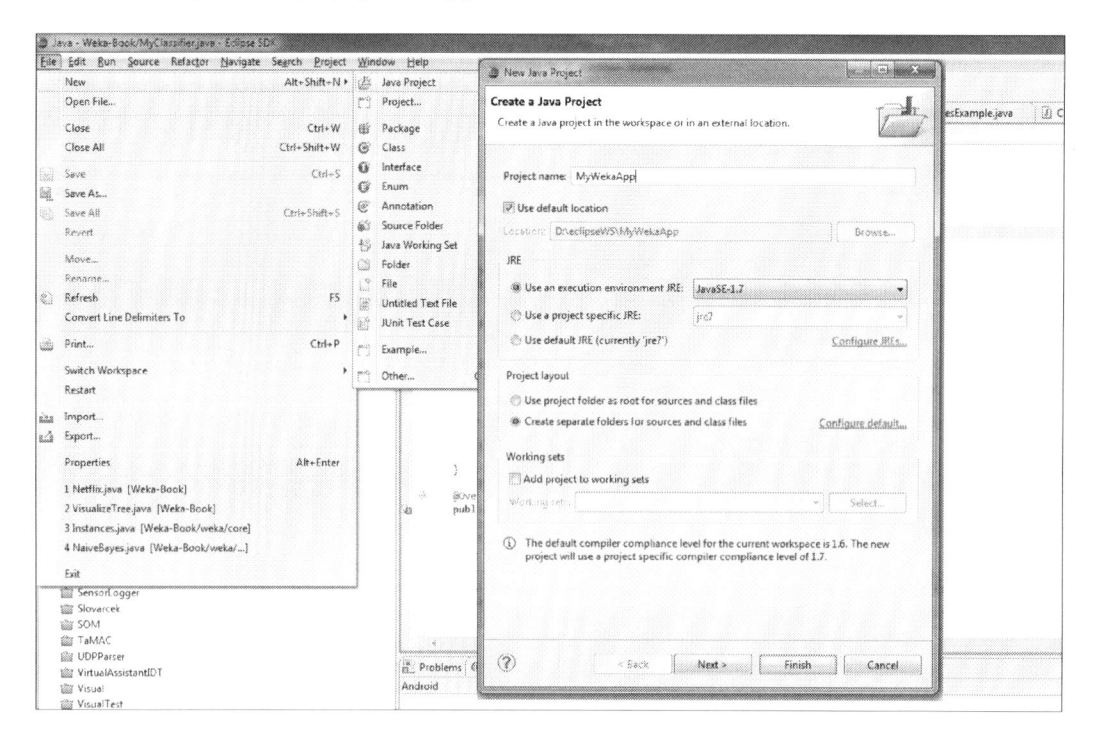

2. Open project properties (right-click on the project MyWekaApp in the package explorer, select **Properties**).

3. Select the **Java Build Path** option from the left panel of the project's **Properties** window.

4. Select **Java Build Path** in the left menu, and choose the **Libraries** tab.
5. Click on **Add External JARs...**.
6. Navigate to the Weka installation folder.

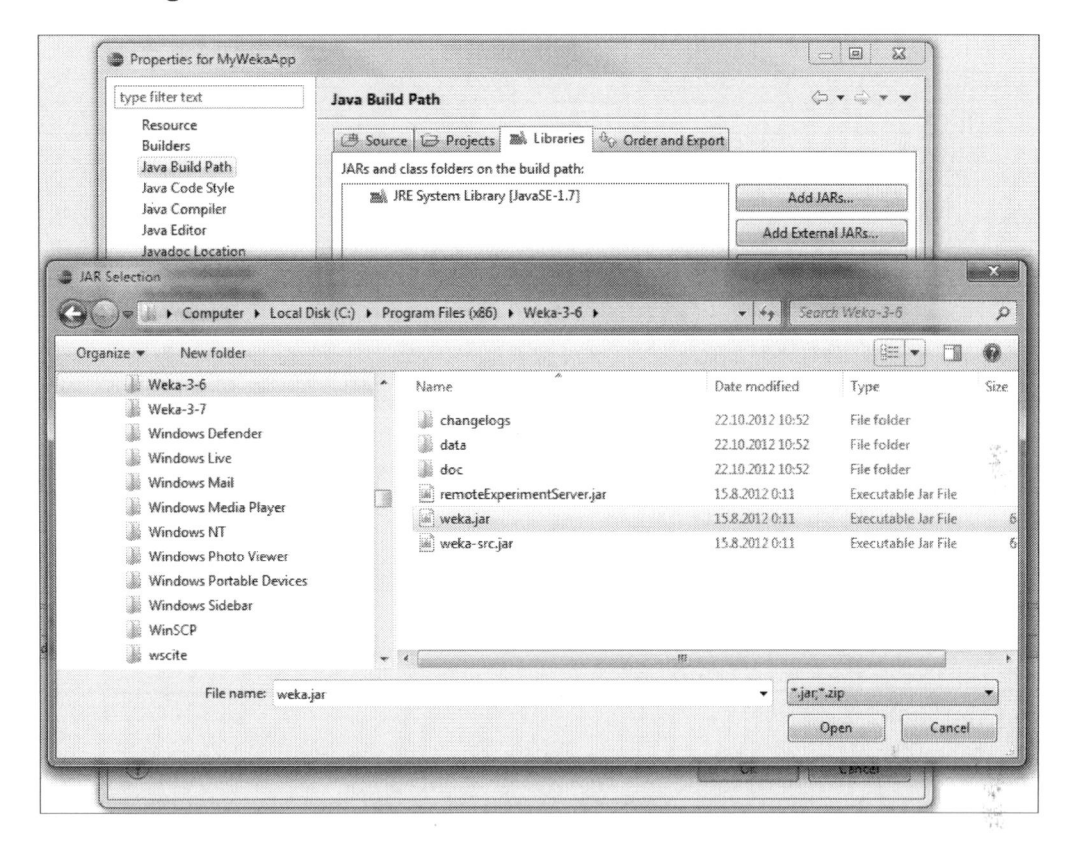

7. Choose the `weka.jar` package and click on **Open** and then **OK**.

Loading the data (Simple)

This task will show you how to load a dataset in **Attribute-Relation File Format** (**ARFF**), typically used to store training and testing data. In addition, it will demonstrate how to create a dataset on the fly and save the data into a file. The detailed ARFF description is available at `http://weka.wikispaces.com/ARFF+(book+version)`.

To demonstrate the recipe, we will use a dataset that describes the fate of the passengers of the ocean liner Titanic. The sinking of the Titanic is a famous event, and many well-known facts—from the proportion of first-class passengers to the "women-and-children-first" policy, and the fact that that policy was not entirely successful in saving the women and children from the third class—are reflected in the survival rates for various classes of passengers.

How to do it...

Use the following snippet (saved in `LoadData.java`) to import a dataset to Weka, print the number of examples in the dataset, and output the complete dataset.

```java
import weka.core.Instances;
import weka.core.converters.ConverterUtils.DataSource;

public class LoadData{
  public static void main(String args[]) throws Exception{
    DataSource source = new DataSource("dataset/titanic.arff");
    Instances data = source.getDataSet();
    System.out.println(data.numInstances()+" instances loaded.");
    System.out.println(data.toString());
  }
}
```

How it works...

Each example in the dataset, represented by a line in the dataset, is handled with an `Instance` object. The complete dataset is handled with the `Instances` object, which can handle an ordered set of weighted instances (used by algorithms that can handle weighted instances, the default weight is 1.0). Hence, we first import the `weka.core.Instances` class with the following command:

```java
import weka.core.Instances;
```

Next, import the `DataSource` class that is able to load a variety of file formats—it is not limited only to ARFF files, but it can also read all file formats that Weka can import via its converters.

```java
import weka.core.converters.ConverterUtils.DataSource;
```

Now, instantiate a `DataSource` object and specify the location of the ARFF file containing the dataset:

```java
DataSource source = new DataSource("dataset/titanic.arff");
```

Call `getDataSet()`, which reads the specified file and returns a new dataset object if the specified ARFF file is valid.

```java
Instances data = source.getDataSet();
```

Finally, we can print the number of records (that is, instances) in our dataset with the `numInstances()` method or list the complete dataset with the `toString()` method.

```java
System.out.println(data.numInstances()+" instances loaded.");
System.out.println(data.toString());
```

There's more...

Sometimes, the data is readily available in real time. In this case, it might be time consuming to make the ARFF files first. This section first demonstrates how to create a dataset on-the-fly and then explains how to save a dataset for later use.

Creating a dataset in runtime

The following lines of code show an example of how to create a dataset at runtime. We will create a dataset describing a basic blog post with attributes such as category, number of visits, title, and date when it was posted.

First, import the following objects:

```
import weka.core.Attribute;
import weka.core.Instance;
import weka.core.Instances;
import weka.core.FastVector;
```

The `Attribute` class contains information about the attribute type (for example, nominal, numeric, or date) and a list of possible values in case the attribute is nominal.

Next, set up attributes with the Weka's `FastVector` class. Weka's data structure is quite similar to Vector in Java:

```
FastVector attributes = new FastVector();
```

To add a nominal attribute such as `category`, first specify all the possible values in a `FastVector` object and then initialize an `Attribute` object with these values:

```
FastVector catVals = new FastVector(3);
  catVals.addElement("sports");
  catVals.addElement("finance");
  catVals.addElement("news");
attributes.addElement(new Attribute("category (att1)", catVals));
```

A numeric attribute is initialized only with the attribute name:

```
attributes.addElement(new Attribute("visits (att2)"));
```

A string attribute is initialized with the null `FastVector` object:

```
attributes.addElement(new Attribute("title (att3)", (FastVector)
null));
```

A date attribute is initialized with the date format string in the ISO-8601 standard (http://www.iso.org/iso/home/standards/iso8601.htm), for example:

```
attributes.addElement(new Attribute("posted (att4)", "yyyy-MM-dd"));
```

After the attributes are initialized, create an empty dataset with them and initial the size to zero:

```
Instances data = new Instances("Runtime dataset", attributes, 0);
```

Next, add some instances by first specifying the instance attribute values and then appending a new `Instance` object to the dataset. Note, that attribute order is important; it must correspond to the order of attributes added to the `data`.

```
double[] vals = new double[data.numAttributes()];
  // nominal value
  vals[0] = data.attribute(0).indexOf("sports");
  // numeric value
  vals[1] = 8527.0;
  // string value
  vals[2] = data.attribute(2).addStringValue("2012 Summer Olympics in London");
  // date value
  vals[3] = data.attribute(3).parseDate("2012-07-27");
data.add(new Instance(1.0, vals));
```

If there is a missing value, you can specify it as follows:

```
vals[3] = Instance.missingValue();
```

Finally, output the data:

```
System.out.println(data.toString());
```

Saving the dataset to ARFF file

This example shows how to save a large dataset in a file. The `toString()` method of the `weka.core.Instances` class does not scale very well for large datasets, since the complete string has to fit into memory. It is best to use a converter which uses an incremental approach for writing the dataset to disk. You should use the `ArffSaver` class (`weka.core.converters.ArffSaver`) for saving a `weka.core.Instances` object to a file.

```
import weka.core.converters.ArffSaver;
import java.io.File;

Instances dataSet = ...
  ArffSaver saver = new ArffSaver();
  saver.setInstances(dataSet);
  saver.setFile(new File("./data/test.arff"));
  saver.writeBatch();
```

Instead of using `saver.writeBatch()`, you can also write the data incrementally yourself as follows:

```
ArffSaver saver = new ArffSaver();
saver.setRetrieval(ArffSaver.INCREMENTAL);
saver.setInstances(dataSet);
saver.setFile(new File("./data/test.arff"));
for(int i=0; i < dataSet.numInstances(); i++){
saver.writeIncremental(data.instance(i));
}
saver.writeIncremental(null);
```

That's it. The dataset is now saved and can be reused, as shown in the recipe.

Filtering attributes (Simple)

A dataset often contains some parts of the data that are not helpful for analysis. One way to get rid of them is to pre-process the dataset and then import it to the Weka. The other way is to remove them after the dataset is loaded in Weka. The supervised filters can take into account the class attribute, while the unsupervised filters disregard it. In addition, filters can perform operation(s) on an attribute or instance that meets filter conditions. These are attribute-based and instance-based filters, respectively. Most filters implement the `OptionHandler` interface allowing you to set the filter options via a `String` array.

This task will demonstrate how to create a filter and apply it on the dataset. Additional sections show a variety of cases such as discretization and classifier-specific filtering.

How to do it...

Before starting, load a dataset, as shown in the previous recipe. Then, to remove, for example, the second attribute from the dataset, use the following code snippet:

```
import weka.core.Instances;
import weka.filters.Filter;
import weka.filters.unsupervised.attribute.Remove;
  ...
String[] opts = new String[]{ "-R", "2"};
Remove remove = new Remove();
remove.setOptions(opts);
remove.setInputFormat(dataset);
Instances newData = Filter.useFilter(dataset, remove);
```

The new dataset is now without the second attribute from the original dataset.

How it works...

First, we import the `Instances` object that holds our dataset.

```
import weka.core.Instances;
```

Next, we import the `Filter` object, which is used to run the selected filter.

```
import weka.filters.Filter;
```

For example, if you want to remove a subset of attributes from the dataset, you need this unsupervised attribute filter

```
weka.filters.unsupervised.attribute.Remove
```

Now, let's construct the `OptionHanlder` interface as a `String` array:

```
String[] options = new String[]{...};
```

The filter documentation specifies the options as follows: specify the range of attributes to act on. This is a comma-separated list of attribute indices, with `first` and `last` valid values. Specify an inclusive range with `-`. For example, `first-3,5,6-10,last`.

Suppose we want to remove the second attribute. Specify that we will use the `Range` parameter and remove the second attribute. The first attribute index is `1`, while `0` is used when a new attribute is created, as shown in the previous recipe.

```
{"-R", "2"}
```

Initialize a new filter instance as follows:

```
Remove remove = new Remove();
```

Pass the options to the newly created filter as follows:

```
remove.setOptions(options);
```

Then pass the original dataset (after setting the options):

```
remove.setInputFormat(dataset);
```

And finally, apply the filter that returns a new dataset:

```
Instances newData = Filter.useFilter(dataset, remove);
```

The new dataset can now be used in other tasks.

There's more...

In addition to the `Remove` filter, we will take a closer look at another important filter; that is, attribute discretization that transforms a real-valued attribute to a nominal-valued attribute. Further, we will demonstrate how to prepare a classifier-specific filter that can apply filtering on the fly.

Attribute discretization

We will first see how an instance filter discretizes a range of numeric attributes in the dataset into nominal attributes.

Use the following code snippet to discretize all the attribute values to binary values:

```
import weka.core.Instances;
import weka.filters.Filter;
import weka.filters.unsupervised.attribute.Discretize;
...
String[] options = new String[4];
```

Specify the number of discrete intervals, for example 2:

```
options[0] = "-B";
options[1] = "2";
```

Specify the range of the attribute on which you want to apply the filter, for example, all the attributes:

```
options[2 = "-R";
options[3 = "first-last";
```

Apply the filter:

```
Discretize discretize = new Discretize();
discretize.setOptions(options);
discretize.setInputFormat(dataset);
Instances newData = Filter.useFilter(dataset, discretize);
```

Classifier-specific filter

An easy way to filter data on the fly is to use the `FilteredClassifier` class. This is a meta-classifier that removes the necessity of filtering the data before training the classifier and prediction. This example demonstrates a meta-classifier with the `Remove` filter and `J48` decision trees for removing the first attribute (it could be, for example, a numeric ID attribute) in the dataset. For additional details on classifiers see the *Training a classifier (Simple)* and *Building your own classifier (Advanced)* recipe, for evaluation see the *Testing and evaluating your models (Simple)* recipe.

Instant Weka How-to

Import the `FilteredClassifier` meta classifier, the `J48` decision trees classifier, and the `Remove` filter:

```
import weka.classifiers.meta.FilteredClassifier;
import weka.classifiers.trees.J48;
import weka.filters.unsupervised.attribute.Remove;
```

Initialize the filter and base classifier:

```
Remove rm = new Remove();
rm.setAttributeIndices("1");
J48 j48 = new J48();
```

Create the `FilteredClassifier` object, specify filter, and base classifier:

```
FilteredClassifier fc = new FilteredClassifier();
fc.setFilter(rm);
fc.setClassifier(j48);
```

Build the meta-classifier:

```
Instances dataset = ...
fc.buildClassifier(dataset);
```

To classify an instance, you can simply use the following:

```
Instance instance = ...
double prediction = fc.classifyInstance(instance);
```

The instance is automatically filtered before classification, in our case, the first attribute is removed.

Selecting attributes (Intermediate)

All the attributes are not always relevant for the classification tasks, in fact, irrelevant attributes can even decrease the performance of some algorithms. This recipe will show you how to find relevant attributes. It will demonstrate how to select an evaluator and a searching method that applies the selected evaluator on the attributes. In Weka, you have three options for performing attribute selection:

- The filter approach (located in `weka.filters.supervised.attribute.AttributeSelection`) that returns a reduced/ranked dataset by applying the filter
- The low-level approach (located in `weka.attributeSelection`), using the attribute selection classes directly outputting some additional useful information
- The meta-classifier approach that combines a search algorithm and evaluator next to a base classifier

Getting ready

Load a dataset as described in the *Loading the data (Simple)* recipe.

How to do it...

To rank a set of attributes, use the following code snippet:

```
import weka.attributeSelection.CfsSubsetEval;
import weka.attributeSelection.GreedyStepwise;
import weka.core.Instances;
import weka.filters.Filter;
import weka.filters.supervised.attribute.AttributeSelection;
...
AttributeSelection filter = new AttributeSelection();  // package
weka.filters.supervised.attribute!
CfsSubsetEval eval = new CfsSubsetEval();
GreedyStepwise search = new GreedyStepwise();
search.setSearchBackwards(true);
filter.setEvaluator(eval);
filter.setSearch(search);
filter.setInputFormat(data);
Instances newData = Filter.useFilter(data, filter);
```

The `newData` variable now contains a dataset containing only relevant attributes according to the selected evaluator.

How it works...

In this example, we will use the filter approach. First, we import the `AttributeSelection` class:

```
import weka.filters.supervised.attribute.AttributeSelection;
```

Next, import an evaluator, for example, correlation-based feature subset selection. This evaluator requires a `GreedyStepwise` search procedure to perform a greedy forward or backward search through the space of attribute subsets. It is implemented in the `GreedyStepwise` class:

```
import weka.attributeSelection.CfsSubsetEval;
import weka.attributeSelection.GreedyStepwise;
```

Import the `Instances` and `Filter` class:

```
import weka.core.Instances;
import weka.filters.Filter;
```

Instant Weka How-to

Create a new `AttributeSelection` object and initialize the evaluator and search algorithm objects:

```
AttributeSelection filter = new AttributeSelection();
CfsSubsetEval eval = new CfsSubsetEval();
GreedyStepwise search = new GreedyStepwise();
```

Set the algorithm to search backward:

```
search.setSearchBackwards(true);
```

Pass the evaluator and search algorithm to the filter:

```
filter.setEvaluator(eval);
filter.setSearch(search);
```

Specify the dataset:

```
filter.setInputFormat(data);
```

Apply the filter:

```
Instances newData = Filter.useFilter(data, filter);
```

In the last step, the greedy algorithm runs with the correlation-based feature selection evaluator to discover a subset of attributes with the highest predictive power. The procedure stops when the addition/deletion of any remaining attributes results in a decrease in evaluation. Attributes not reaching a default threshold may be discarded from the ranking (you can manually set this by the `filter.setThreshold(...)` method).

There's more...

This section will first demonstrate an alternative, yet popular, measure for attribute selection, that is, information gain. Next, we will take a look at how to reduce the attribute space dimensionality using the principle component analysis. Finally, we will show how to select attributes on the fly.

Select attributes using information gain

As seen in the recipe, a filter is directly applied to the dataset, so there is no need to manually remove attributes later. This example shows how to apply a low-level approach, if the previous method is not suitable for your purposes.

In this case, we import the actual attribute selection classes (in the previous example, we imported filters based on this class):

```
import weka.attributeSelection.AttributeSelection
```

Create a new `AtributeSelection` instance:

```
AttributeSelection attSelect = new AttributeSelection();
```

Initialize a measure for ranking attributes, for example, information gain:

```
InfoGainAttributeEval eval = new InfoGainAttributeEval();
```

Specify the search method as `Ranker`, as the name suggests it simply ranks the attributes by a selected measure:

```
Ranker search = new Ranker();
```

Load the measure and search method to the attribute selection object:

```
attSelect.setEvaluator(eval);
attSelect.setSearch(search);
```

Perform the attribute selection with the particular search method and measure using the specified dataset:

```
attSelect.SelectAttributes(data);
```

Print the results as follows:

```
System.out.println(attSelect.toResultsString());
```

Get, and print, the indices of the selected attributes:

```
int[] indices = attSelect.selectedAttributes();
System.out.println(Utils.arrayToString(indices));
```

The output, for example, for the titanic dataset is:

```
=== Attribute Selection on all input data ===

Search Method:
    Attribute ranking.

Attribute Evaluator (supervised, Class (nominal): 4 survived):
    Information Gain Ranking Filter

Ranked attributes:
 0.14239    3 sex
 0.05929    1 class
 0.00641    2 age

Selected attributes: 3,1,2 : 3
```

The information gain ranker selected the first three attributes, indicating their importance.

Principal component analysis

Principal component analysis (**PCA**) is a dimensionality reduction technique often used to represent the dataset with less attributes while preserving as much information as possible. Dimensionality reduction is accomplished by choosing enough eigenvectors to account for a percentage of the variance in the original data (the default is 95 percent). This example shows how to transform the dataset to a new coordinate system defined by the principal eigenvectors.

```
import weka.filters.supervised.attribute.AttributeSelection;
...
AttributeSelection filter = new AttributeSelection();
```

Initialize the principal components evaluator:

```
PrincipalComponents eval = new PrincipalComponents();
```

Initialize ranker as a search method:

```
Ranker search = new Ranker();
```

Set the evaluator and search method, filter the data, and print the newly created dataset in a new coordinate system:

```
filter.setEvaluator(eval);
filter.setSearch(search);
filter.setInputFormat(data);
Instances newData = Filter.useFilter(data, filter);
System.out.println(newData);
```

The new dataset is now represented by values in a new, smaller coordinate system, which means there are less attributes.

Classifier-specific selection

This example shows how to work with a class for running an arbitrary classifier on data that has been reduced through attribute selection.

Import the `AttributeSelectedClassifier` class:

```
import weka.classifiers.meta.AttributeSelectedClassifier;
```

Create a new object:

```
AttributeSelectedClassifier classifier = new
AttributeSelectedClassifier();
```

Initialize an evaluator, for example, `ReliefF`, which requires the `Ranker` search algorithm:

```
ReliefFAttributeEval eval = new ReliefFAttributeEval();
Ranker search = new Ranker();
```

Initialize a base classifier, for example, decision trees:

```
J48 baseClassifier = new J48();
```

Pass the base classifier, evaluator, and search algorithm to the meta-classifier:

```
classifier.setClassifier(baseClassifier);
classifier.setEvaluator(eval);
classifier.setSearch(search);
```

Finally, run and validate the classifier, for example, with 10-fold-cross validation (see *Classification* recipe for details):

```
Evaluation evaluation = new Evaluation(data);
evaluation.crossValidateModel(classifier, data, 10, new Random(1));
System.out.println(evaluation.toSummaryString());
```

The evaluation outputs the classifier performance on a set of attributes reduced by the `ReliefF` ranker.

Training a classifier (Simple)

The most exciting task in data mining is classifier training. This recipe will show you how to train a classifier and set the options.

Getting ready

Load a dataset as described in the *Loading the data (Simple)* recipe.

How to do it...

To train a classifier, use the following snippet:

```
import weka.classifiers.trees.J48;

String[] options = new String[1];
options[0] = "-U";
J48 tree = new J48();
tree.setOptions(options);
tree.buildClassifier(data);
```

The classifier is now trained and ready for classification.

How it works...

The classifier implements the `OptionHandler` interface, which allows you to set the options via a `String` array. First, import a classifier from the `weka.classifiers` package, for example, a `J48` decision tree:

```
import weka.classifiers.trees.J48;
```

Then, prepare the options in a String array, for example, set the tree to be unpruned:

```
String[] options = new String[1];
options[0] = "-U";            // un-pruned tree
```

Now, initialize the classifier:

```
J48 tree = new J48();         // new instance of tree
```

Set the options with the `OptionHandler` interface:

```
tree.setOptions(options);     // set the options
```

And build the classifier:

```
tree.buildClassifier(data);   // build classifier
```

Now, you are ready to validate it and use it (see recipes *Test* and *Evaluate*).

There's more...

There is a wide variety of implemented classifiers in Weka. This section first demonstrates how to build a support vector machine classifier, and then it lists some other popular classifiers, and finally it shows how to create a classifier that is able to incrementally accept data.

Support vector machine

Another popular classifier is support vector machine. To train one, follow the previous recipe but instead of `J48`, import the `SMO` class from `weka.classifiers.functions`:

```
import weka.classifiers.functions.SMO;
```

Then, initialize a new object and build the classifier:

```
SMO svm = new SMO();
svm.buildClassifier(data);
```

Other classification models

In addition to decision trees (`weka.classifiers.trees.J48`) and support vector machines (`weka.classifiers.functions.SMO`), we have listed some of the many other classification algorithms one can use in Weka:

- `weka.classifiers.rules.ZeroR`: Predicts the majority class (mode) and it is considered as a baseline; that is, if your classifier's performance is worse than the average value predictor, it is not worth considering it.
- `weka.classifiers.trees.RandomTree`: Constructs a tree that considers *K* randomly chosen attributes at each node.
- `weka.classifiers.trees.RandomForest`: Constructs a set (that is, forest) of random trees and uses majority voting to classify a new instance.
- `weka.classifiers.lazy.IBk`: *K*-nearest neighbors classifier that is able to select appropriate value of neighbors based on cross-validation.
- `weka.classifiers.functions.MultilayerPerceptron`: A classifier based on neural networks that uses back-propagation to classify instances. The network can be built by hand, or created by an algorithm, or both.
- `weka.classifiers.bayes.NaiveBayes`: A naive Bayes classifier that uses estimator classes, where numeric estimator precision values are chosen based on analysis of the training data.
- `weka.classifiers.meta.AdaBoostM1`: The class for boosting a nominal class classifier using the Adaboost M1 method. Only nominal class problems can be tackled. Often dramatically improves performance, but sometimes overfits.
- `weka.classifiers.meta.Bagging`: The class for bagging a classifier to reduce variance. Can do classification and regression depending on the base learner.

Incremental classifiers

When a dataset is really big or you have to deal with real-time, stream data, then the preceding methods won't fit into memory all at once. Some classifiers implement the `weka.classifiers.UpdateableClassifier` interface, which means they can be trained incrementally. These are `AODE`, `IB1`, `IBk`, `KStar`, `LWL`, `NaiveBayesUpdateable`, `NNge`, `RacedIncrementalLogitBoost`, and `Winnow`.

The process of training an incremental classifier with the `UpdatableClassifier` interface is fairly simple.

Open a dataset with the `ArffLoader` class:

```
ArffLoader loader = new ArffLoader();
loader.setFile(new File("/some/where/data.arff"));
```

Load the structure of the dataset (does not contain any actual data rows):

```
Instances data = loader.getStructure();
data.setClassIndex(structure.numAttributes() - 1);
```

Initialize a classifier and call `buildClassifier` with the structure of the dataset:

```
NaiveBayesUpdateable nb = new NaiveBayesUpdateable();
nb.buildClassifier(structure);
```

Subsequently, call the `updateClassifier` method to feed the classifier new `weka.core.Instance` objects, one by one:

```
Instance current;
while ((current = loader.getNextInstance(structure)) != null)
   nb.updateClassifier(current);
```

After each update, the classifier takes into account the newly added instance to update its model.

Building your own classifier (Advanced)

This recipe will show you how to build your own classifier. It will cover the most essential steps required to design a functional classifier. We will create a classifier that takes instances with numeric or nominal attributes and nominal class value(s). The prediction will be simple: the class value of a new instance will be predicted as the class value of the second nearest neighbor (in case there are more neighbors with the same distance, it will just take the first one). To make this work, the classifier will need at least two learning examples.

How to do it...

To build a classifier, we have to extend the `weka.classifiers.Classifier` class, as shown in the following snippet:

```
import java.util.Enumeration;

import weka.classifiers.Classifier;
import weka.core.Capabilities;
import weka.core.Capabilities.Capability;
import weka.core.Instance;
import weka.core.Instances;

public class MyClassifier extends Classifier {

   private Instances trainData;
```

```java
public Capabilities getCapabilities() {

  Capabilities result = super.getCapabilities();
  result.disableAll();

  result.enable(Capability.NUMERIC_ATTRIBUTES);
  result.enable(Capability.NOMINAL_ATTRIBUTES);
  result.enable(Capability.NOMINAL_CLASS);
  result.setMinimumNumberInstances(2);

  return result;
}

@Override
public void buildClassifier(Instances data) throws Exception {

  getCapabilities().testWithFail(data);
  data = new Instances(data);
  data.deleteWithMissingClass();
  Instances trainData = new Instances(data, 0, data.numInstances());

}

public double classifyInstance(Instance instance) {

  double minDistance = Double.MAX_VALUE;
  double secondMinDistance = Double.MAX_VALUE;
  double distance;
  double classVal = 0, minClassVal = 0;

  Enumeration enu = trainData.enumerateInstances();
  while (enu.hasMoreElements()) {

    Instance trainInstance = (Instance) enu.nextElement();
    if (!trainInstance.classIsMissing()) {

      distance = distance(instance, trainInstance);

      if (distance < minDistance) {

        secondMinDistance = minDistance;
        minDistance = distance;

        classVal = minClassVal;
```

```
                minClassVal = trainInstance.classValue();

            } else if (distance < secondMinDistance) {
                secondMinDistance = distance;
                classVal = trainInstance.classValue();
            }
          }
        }
        return classVal;
      }
    }
```

The `MyClassifier` class can now be used as described in the *Training a classifier (Simple)* recipe.

How it works...

Each classifier extends the `weka.classifiers.Classifier` abstract class, hence we first import:

```
import java.util.Enumeration;
```

Next, to define what kind of magic powers our classifier can possess, we need the `weka.core.Capabilities` class and some constants from the same class:

```
import weka.core.Capabilities;
import weka.core.Capabilities.Capability;
```

Import the `Instance` and `Instances` class

```
import weka.core.Instance;
import weka.core.Instances;
```

Create a new class with your classifier name that extends the `weka.classifiers.Classifier` abstract class. If you also want your classifier to be incremental (as shown in the previous example), make sure you implement the `weka.classifiers.UpdateableClassifier` interface and the `updateClassifier(Instance instance)` method.

```
public class MyClassifier extends Classifier {
Initialize a private variable to store classifier's train dataset
    private Instances trainData;
```

Now, specify what kind of data your classifier is able to handle in the `getCapabilities()` method.

```
    public Capabilities getCapabilities() {
```

First, inherit all possible capabilities a classifier can handle and, by default, disable all of them to avoid surprises later.

```
Capabilities result = super.getCapabilities();
result.disableAll();
```

We want our classifier to be able to handle numeric and nominal attributes only. Enable them by setting the following constants from the `weka.core.Capabilities.Capability` class using `enable(enum Capability)` method.

```
result.enable(Capability.NUMERIC_ATTRIBUTES);
result.enable(Capability.NOMINAL_ATTRIBUTES);
```

Next, enable your classifier to handle nominal class values:

```
result.enable(Capability.NOMINAL_CLASS);
```

Specify that it needs at least two training instances with the `setMinimumNumberInstances(int)` method:

```
result.setMinimumNumberInstances(2);
```

Finally, return the capabilities object:

```
    return result;
}
```

The next underpinning component of your classifier is `buildClassifier(Instances)` method. This is where usually most of the hard work is done to create a model, for example, a decision tree or SVM vectors. Our classifier is an exception from the family of lazy classifiers, which passes all the hard work to the `classifyInstance(Instance)` method as we will see later.

```
@Override
public void buildClassifier(Instances data) throws Exception {
```

First, check if the passed train dataset is in compliance with the capabilities defined previously.

```
    getCapabilities().testWithFail(data);
```

Next, copy the complete dataset and remove the instances with missing class values using the `deleteWithMissingClass()` method, since they are not useful for classification:

```
    // remove instances with missing class
    data = new Instances(data);
    data.deleteWithMissingClass();
```

Instant Weka How-to

Now, we are ready to do the hard work of building an actual model. Well, our lazy classifiers simply remember the training data and this is it. If your classifier is not as lazy as this one, then this is a good place to implement it.

```
        trainData = new Instances(data, 0, data.numInstances());
    }
```

OK, we have built the model, and the last missing part is the `double classifyInstance(Instance instance)` method that predicts a class value of a given instance. Note, that it actually returns an index (as double) of the nominal value in the class attribute. The following method simply finds an instance with the second closest distance. The distance method itself is implemented as follows:

```
    public double classifyInstance(Instance instance) {

        double minDistance = Double.MAX_VALUE;
        double secondMinDistance = Double.MAX_VALUE;
        double distance;
        double classVal = 0, minClassVal = 0;

        Enumeration enu = trainData.enumerateInstances();
        while (enu.hasMoreElements()) {

          Instance trainInstance = (Instance) enu.nextElement();
          if (!trainInstance.classIsMissing()) {

            distance = distance(instance, trainInstance);

            if (distance < minDistance) {

              secondMinDistance = minDistance;
              minDistance = distance;

              classVal = minClassVal;
              minClassVal = trainInstance.classValue();

            } else if (distance < secondMinDistance) {
              secondMinDistance = distance;
              classVal = trainInstance.classValue();
            }
          }
        }
        return classVal;

    }
```

The `distance(Instance, Instance)` method demonstrates a basic approach of how to measure the difference between two instances. It performs any attribute normalization. The main idea is to summarize the difference by corresponding attributes excluding class value. Since our classifier also supports nominal attribute values, we simply use **Hamming distance**. The source code can be found in code bundle.

Tree visualization (Intermediate)

Decision trees can be extremely helpful to understand the underlying patterns in the dataset when visualized. This recipe demonstrates how to visualize a `J48` decision tree. We will load our Titanic dataset, build a tree, and visualize it in a frame.

How to do it...

To visualize a tree, run this snippet:

```java
import java.awt.BorderLayout;
import java.io.BufferedReader;
import java.io.FileReader;

import weka.classifiers.trees.J48;
import weka.core.Instances;
import weka.gui.treevisualizer.PlaceNode2;
import weka.gui.treevisualizer.TreeVisualizer;

...
Instances data = new Instances(new BufferedReader(new
FileReader(dataset)));
data.setClassIndex(data.numAttributes() - 1);

J48 classifier = new J48();
classifier.buildClassifier(data);


TreeVisualizer tv = new TreeVisualizer(null, classifier.graph(), new
PlaceNode2());

JFrame frame = new javax.swing.JFrame("Tree Visualizer");
frame.setSize(800, 500);
frame.setDefaultCloseOperation(JFrame.EXIT_ON_CLOSE);

frame.getContentPane().add(tv);
frame.setVisible(true);

tv.fitToScreen();
```

How it works...

Import the J48 classifier and the weka.core.Instances class:

```
import weka.classifiers.trees.J48;
import weka.core.Instances;
```

From weka.gui.treevisualizer first import the PlaceNode2 class that places the nodes of a tree so that they fall evenly below their parent without overlapping.

```
import weka.gui.treevisualizer.PlaceNode2;
```

Next, from the same package, import TreeVisualizer, which displays the node structure in Swing:

```
import weka.gui.treevisualizer.TreeVisualizer;
```

Then, load a dataset:

```
Instances data = new Instances(new BufferedReader(new FileReader(dataset)));
data.setClassIndex(data.numAttributes() - 1);
```

Build a classifier:

```
J48 classifier = new J48();
classifier.buildClassifier(data);
```

Call the TreeVisualizer(TreeDisplayListener tdl, String dot, NodePlace p) constructor. It expects a listener (null in our case), a tree provided in dot format (generated by classifier.graph()), and an algorithm to place the nodes (PlaceNode2):

```
TreeVisualizer tv = new TreeVisualizer(null, classifier.graph(), new PlaceNode2());
```

Create a frame:

```
JFrame frame = new javax.swing.JFrame("Tree Visualizer");
frame.setSize(800, 500);
frame.setDefaultCloseOperation(JFrame.EXIT_ON_CLOSE);
```

Add tree visualizer to the content pane:

```
frame.getContentPane().add(tv);
```

Make the frame visible:

```
frame.setVisible(true);
```

And call the `fitToScreen()` method to resize the tree:

```
tv.fitToScreen();
```

The result is a frame:

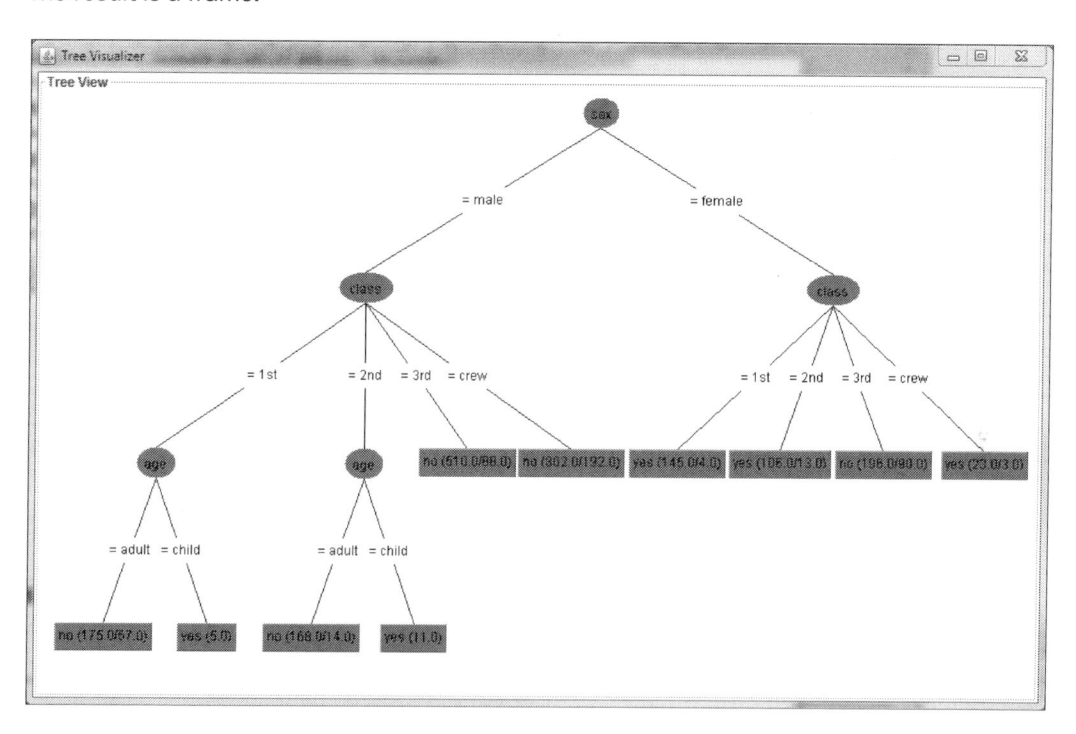

Testing and evaluating your models (Simple)

In order to trust a model, it is necessary to provide its performance, that is, how accurate the model is when making its classifications. This recipe will show you how to assess the performance using a variety of measures and different evaluation techniques such as separated train and test dataset, and K-fold cross validation.

How to do it...

We will use the `J48` decision trees classifier and demonstrate 10-fold cross validation on the Titanic dataset using the following code snippet:

```
import weka.core.Instances;
import weka.core.converters.ConverterUtils.DataSource;
import weka.classifiers.Evaluation;
import weka.classifiers.trees.J48;
```

```
...
DataSource source = new DataSource("dataset/titanic.arff");

Instances data = source.getDataSet();
data.setClassIndex(data.numAttributes() - 1);
J48 classifier = new J48();

Evaluation eval = new Evaluation(data);
eval.crossValidateModel(classifier, data, 10, new Random(1));

System.out.println(eval.toSummaryString("Results\n ", false));
```

You should be able to see the following output:

```
Results
Correctly Classified Instances        1737             78.9187 %
Incorrectly Classified Instances       464             21.0813 %
Kappa statistic                          0.429
Mean absolute error                      0.312
Root mean squared error                  0.3959
Relative absolute error                 71.3177 %
Root relative squared error             84.6545 %
Coverage of cases (0.95 level)          99.7274 %
Mean rel. region size (0.95 level)      96.3426 %
Total Number of Instances             2201
```

The output shows various performance measures. Note, that some measures make sense only for the numeric class (for example, mean absolute and root mean squared error), while other only for nominal class (correctly and incorrectly classified instances).

How it works...

First, load the titanic data.

```
DataSource source = new DataSource("dataset/titanic.arff");
Instances data = source.getDataSet();
```

Set the last attribute as class.

```
data.setClassIndex(data.numAttributes() - 1);
```

Initialize a classifier that will be evaluated.

```
J48 classifier = new J48();
```

Initialize the `weka.classifiers.Evaluation` class with the dataset structure.

```
Evaluation eval = new Evaluation(data);
```

Perform cross validation using the selected classifier, 10-folds split, and random seed that is used to split folds (for debugging make sure the random seed is constant).

```
eval.crossValidateModel(classifier, data, 10, new Random(1));
```

Finally, print the results:

```
System.out.println(eval.toSummaryString("Results\n", false));
```

There's more...

This section will demonstrate alternative evaluation approaches such as separated train and test set, as well as other performance measures and techniques such as confusion matrix and ROC curve.

Train and test set

In case you have a dedicated test set, you can train the classifier and then evaluate it on this test set. In the following example, a J48 is instantiated, trained, and then evaluated.

```
import weka.core.Instances;
import weka.classifiers.Evaluation;
import weka.classifiers.trees.J48;
```

Load train and test datasets from somewhere:

```
Instances train = ...
Instances test = ...
```

Initialize and build the classifier:

```
Classifier cls = new J48();
cls.buildClassifier(train);
```

Initialize evaluation with the train dataset structure:

```
Evaluation eval = new Evaluation(train);
```

Evaluate the built classifier with the test dataset:

```
eval.evaluateModel(cls, test);
```

Print statistics:

```
System.out.println(eval.toSummaryString("Results\n", false));
```

The outputted measures are the same as in the cross-validation case.

Other statistics

You can also retrieve specific results from the evaluation object as follows:

- Number of correctly classified instances (nominal class, see also the `incorrect()` method):

    ```
    System.out.println(eval.correct());
    ```

- The percentage of correctly classified instances (nominal class):

    ```
    System.out.println(eval.pctCorrect());
    ```

- Kappa statistics (nominal class):

    ```
    System.out.println(eval.kappa());
    ```

- Percentage of unclassified instances (nominal class):

    ```
    System.out.println(eval.pctUnclassified());
    ```

- Number of unclassified instances (nominal class):

    ```
    System.out.println(eval.unclassified());
    ```

- The root mean squared error:

    ```
    System.out.println(eval.rootMeanSquaredError());
    ```

- The mean absolute error:

    ```
    System.out.println(eval.meanAbsoluteError());
    ```

- Correlation coefficient (numeric class):

    ```
    System.out.println(eval.correlationCoefficient());
    ```

Confusion matrix

The confusion matrix simply outputs with the `toMatrixString()` or `toMatrixString(String)` method of the `Evaluation` class:

```
eval.evaluateModel(cls, test);
System.out.println(eval.toMatrixString());
```

It outputs:

```
=== Confusion Matrix ===

    a    b   <-- classified as
  267  444 |    a = yes
   20 1470 |    b = no
```

The confusion matrix can be used to compute additional performance measures such as recall, f-measure, and so on.

ROC curve

To demonstrate how to generate and display an ROC curve from a dataset we will use a default `J48` classifier and titanic dataset:

```
import weka.core.Instances;
import weka.core.converters.ConverterUtils.DataSource;
import weka.classifiers.Evaluation;
import weka.classifiers.trees.J48;
import java.util.Random;
import javax.swing.*;
import weka.core.*;
import weka.classifiers.*;
import weka.classifiers.evaluation.*;
import weka.gui.visualize.*;
...

// load data
DataSource source = new DataSource(dataset);
Instances data = source.getDataSet();
data.setClassIndex(data.numAttributes() - 1);

// train classifier
Classifier cl = new J48();
Evaluation eval = new Evaluation(data);
eval.crossValidateModel(cl, data, 10, new Random(1));

// generate curve
ThresholdCurve tc = new ThresholdCurve();
int classIndex = 0;
Instances result = tc.getCurve(eval.predictions(), classIndex);

// plot curve
ThresholdVisualizePanel vmc = new ThresholdVisualizePanel();
vmc.setROCString("(Area under ROC = "+ Utils.doubleToString(tc.
getROCArea(result), 4) + ")");
vmc.setName(result.relationName());
PlotData2D tempd = new PlotData2D(result);
tempd.setPlotName(result.relationName());
tempd.addInstanceNumberAttribute();
// specify which points are connected
boolean[] cp = new boolean[result.numInstances()];
for (int n = 1; n < cp.length; n++)
  cp[n] = true;
tempd.setConnectPoints(cp);
```

```
// add plot
vmc.addPlot(tempd);

// display curve
JFrame frame = new javax.swing.JFrame("ROC Curve");
frame.setSize(800, 500);
frame.setDefaultCloseOperation(JFrame.EXIT_ON_CLOSE);
frame.getContentPane().add(vmc);
frame.setVisible(true);
```

This outputs the following frame:

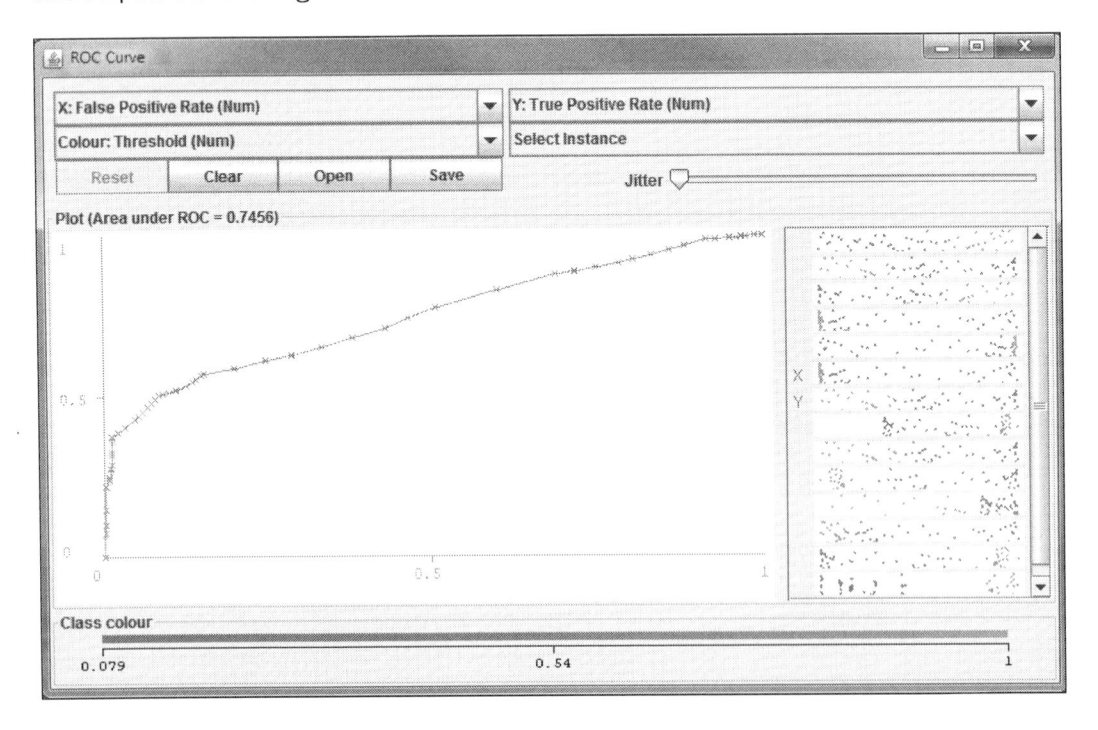

Regression models (Simple)

Regression is a technique used to predict a value of a numerical class, in contrast to classification, which predicts the value of a nominal class. Given a set of attributes, the regression builds a model, usually an equation that is used to compute the predicted class value.

Getting ready

Let's look at an example of a house price-based regression model, and create some real data to examine. These are actual numbers from houses for sale, and we will be trying to find the value of a house we are supposed to sell:

Size (m2)	Land (m2)	Rooms	Granite	Extra bathroom	Price
1076	2801	6	0	0	€324.500,00
990	3067	5	1	1	€466.000,00
1229	3094	5	0	1	€425.900,00
731	4315	4	1	0	€387.120,00
671	2926	4	0	1	€312.100,00
1078	6094	6	1	1	€603.000,00
909	2854	5	0	1	€383.400,00
975	2947	5	1	1	??

To load files in Weka, we have to put the table in the ARFF file format and save it as `house.arff`. Make sure the attributes are numeric, as shown here:

```
@RELATION house
@ATTRIBUTE size NUMERIC
@ATTRIBUTE land NUMERIC
@ATTRIBUTE rooms NUMERIC
@ATTRIBUTE granite NUMERIC
@ATTRIBUTE extra_bathroom NUMERIC
@ATTRIBUTE price NUMERIC

@DATA
1076,2801,6,0,0,324500
990,3067,5,1,1,466000
1229,3094,5,0,1,425900
731,4315,4,1,0,387120
671,2926,4,0,1,312100
1078,6094,6,1,1,603000
909,2854,5,0,1,383400
975,2947,5,1,1,?
```

How to do it...

Use the following snippet:

```java
import java.io.BufferedReader;
import java.io.FileReader;

import weka.core.Instance;
import weka.core.Instances;
import weka.classifiers.functions.LinearRegression;

public class Regression{

  public static void main(String args[]) throws Exception{
    //load data
    Instances data = new Instances(new BufferedReader(new FileReader("dataset/house.arff")));
    data.setClassIndex(data.numAttributes() - 1);

    //build model
    LinearRegression model = new LinearRegression();
    model.buildClassifier(data); //the last instance with missing class is not used
    System.out.println(model);

    //classify the last instance
    Instance myHouse = data.lastInstance();
    double price = model.classifyInstance(myHouse);
    System.out.println("My house ("+myHouse+"): "+price);
  }
}
```

Here is the output:

```
Linear Regression Model

price =

     195.2035 * size +
      38.9694 * land +
   76218.4642 * granite +
   73947.2118 * extra_bathroom +
    2681.136

My house (975,2947,5,1,1,?): 458013.16703945777
```

The model estimated the value of our house to be $458,013.17.

How it works...

Import a basic regression model named `weka.classifiers.functions.LinearRegression`:

```
import java.io.BufferedReader;
import java.io.FileReader;

import weka.core.Instance;
import weka.core.Instances;
import weka.classifiers.functions.LinearRegression;
```

Load the house dataset:

```
Instances data = new Instances(new BufferedReader(new
FileReader("dataset/house.arff")));
data.setClassIndex(data.numAttributes() - 1);
```

Initialize and build a regression model. Note, that the last instance is not used for building the model since the class value is missing:

```
LinearRegression model = new LinearRegression();
model.buildClassifier(data);
```

Output the model:

```
System.out.println(model);
```

Use the model to predict the price of the last instance in the dataset:

```
Instance myHouse = data.lastInstance();
double price = model.classifyInstance(myHouse);
System.out.println("My house ("+myHouse+"): "+price);
```

There's more...

This section lists some additional algorithms.

Other regression algorithms

There is a wide variety of implemented regression algorithms one can use in Weka:

- `weka.classifiers.rules.ZeroR`: The class for building and using an 0-R classifier. Predicts the mean (for a numeric class) or the mode (for a nominal class) and it is considered as a baseline; that is, if your classifier's performance is worse than **average value predictor**, it is not worth considering it.

- `weka.classifiers.trees.REPTree`: The fast decision tree learner. Builds a decision/regression tree using information gain/variance and prunes it using reduced-error pruning (with backfitting). It only sorts values for numeric attributes once. Missing values are dealt with by splitting the corresponding instances into pieces (that is, as in C4.5).

- `weka.classifiers.functions.SMOreg`: SMOreg implements the support vector machine for regression. The parameters can be learned using various algorithms. The algorithm is selected by setting the `RegOptimizer`. The most popular algorithm (`RegSMOImproved`) is due to Shevade, Keerthi, and others, and this is the default `RegOptimizer`.

- `weka.classifiers.functions.MultilayerPerceptron`: A classifier that uses backpropagation to classify instances. This network can be built by hand, or created by an algorithm, or both. The network can also be monitored and modified during training time. The nodes in this network are all sigmoid (except for when the class is numeric in which case the output nodes become unthresholded linear units).

- `weka.classifiers.functions.GaussianProcesses`: Implements Gaussian Processes for regression without hyperparameter-tuning.

Association rules (Intermediate)

Association analysis is used for finding frequent patterns, associations, correlations, or causal structures among sets of items or objects in transaction databases, relational databases, and so on. It's often used to do market basket analysis, as done by big supermarket chains to decide what products are often bought together; these are then placed close to each other in the store to increase the chance of people picking them up on impulse. This recipe will follow you through the initialization of association rules analysis.

Getting ready

This recipe will use a different sample dataset referred to as the bank data, available in a comma-separated format on the Weka website. To illustrate the basic concepts of association rule mining, you can find pre-processed data in the source code bundle located in `/dataset/bank-data.arff`, which is already converted to the ARFF format and filtered.

How to do it...

We will use the Apriori algorithm as implemented in Weka. It iteratively reduces the minimum support until it finds the required number of rules with the given minimum confidence:

```
import java.io.BufferedReader;
import java.io.FileReader;

import weka.core.Instances;
```

```java
import weka.associations.Apriori;

public class AssociationRules{

   public static void main(String args[]) throws Exception{

      //load data
      Instances data = new Instances(new BufferedReader(new
   FileReader("dataset/bank-data.arff")));

      //build model
      Apriori model = new Apriori();
      model.buildAssociations(data);
      System.out.println(model);

   }
}
```

This should output the following:

```
Apriori
=======

Minimum support: 0.1 (60 instances)
Minimum metric <confidence>: 0.9
Number of cycles performed: 18

Generated sets of large itemsets:

Size of set of large itemsets L(1): 28

Size of set of large itemsets L(2): 232

Size of set of large itemsets L(3): 524

Size of set of large itemsets L(4): 277

Size of set of large itemsets L(5): 33
```

Best rules found:

```
   1. income=43759_max 80 ==> save_act=YES 80    <conf:(1)> lift:(1.45)
lev:(0.04) [24] conv:(24.8)
   2. age=52_max income=43759_max 76 ==> save_act=YES 76    <conf:(1)>
lift:(1.45) lev:(0.04) [23] conv:(23.56)
```

```
   3. income=43759_max current_act=YES 63 ==> save_act=YES 63
<conf:(1)> lift:(1.45) lev:(0.03) [19] conv:(19.53)
   4. age=52_max income=43759_max current_act=YES 61 ==> save_act=YES 61
<conf:(1)> lift:(1.45) lev:(0.03) [18] conv:(18.91)
   5. children=0 save_act=YES mortgage=NO pep=NO 74 ==> married=YES 73
<conf:(0.99)> lift:(1.49) lev:(0.04) [24] conv:(12.58)
   6. sex=FEMALE children=0 mortgage=NO pep=NO 64 ==> married=YES 63
<conf:(0.98)> lift:(1.49) lev:(0.03) [20] conv:(10.88)
   7. children=0 current_act=YES mortgage=NO pep=NO 82 ==> married=YES
80    <conf:(0.98)> lift:(1.48) lev:(0.04) [25] conv:(9.29)
   8. children=0 mortgage=NO pep=NO 107 ==> married=YES 104
<conf:(0.97)> lift:(1.47) lev:(0.06) [33] conv:(9.1)
   9. income=43759_max current_act=YES 63 ==> age=52_max 61
<conf:(0.97)> lift:(3.04) lev:(0.07) [40] conv:(14.32)
   10. income=43759_max save_act=YES current_act=YES 63 ==> age=52_max 61
<conf:(0.97)> lift:(3.04) lev:(0.07) [40] conv:(14.32)
```

The algorithm outputs a set of rules describing interesting patterns.

How it works...

Import the `weka.associations.Apriori` class implementing the `Apriori` algorithm:

```
import weka.associations.Apriori;

public class AssociationRules{

  public static void main(String args[]) throws Exception{
```

Load the bank dataset:

```
    Instances data = new Instances(new BufferedReader(new FileReader("dataset/bank-data.arff")));
```

Initialize the `Apriori` algorithm:

```
    Apriori model = new Apriori();
```

Call the `buildAssociations(Instances)` method to trigger the association rule discovery procedure:

```
    model.buildAssociations(data);
```

Finally, output the discovered rules:

```
    System.out.println(model);
```

The output is interpreted as follows. Consider the sixth rule:

```
6. sex=FEMALE children=0 mortgage=NO pep=NO 64 ==> married=YES 63
   <conf:(0.98)> lift:(1.49) lev:(0.03) [20] conv:(10.88)
```

The first part corresponds to the discovered rule/pattern, which is based on 64 examples and supported by 63 of them:

```
sex=FEMALE children=0 mortgage=NO pep=NO 64 ==> married=YES 63
```

Clustering (Simple)

This recipe will demonstrate how to perform basic clustering. We will again use the bank data introduced in the previous recipe.

Getting ready

The idea of clustering is to automatically group examples in the dataset by a similarity measure, most commonly by Euclidean distance.

How to do it...

Execute the following code:

```java
import java.io.BufferedReader;
import java.io.FileReader;

import weka.core.Instances;
import weka.clusterers.EM;

public class Clustering {

  public static void main(String args[]) throws Exception{

    //load data
    Instances data = new Instances(new BufferedReader(new FileReader("dataset/bank-data.arff")));

    // new instance of clusterer
    EM model = new EM();
    // build the clusterer
    model.buildClusterer(data);
    System.out.println(model);

  }
}
```

Here is the output:

```
EM
==

Number of clusters selected by cross validation: 6

                    Cluster
Attribute             0        1        2        3        4        5
                    (0.1)   (0.13)   (0.26)   (0.25)   (0.12)   (0.14)
=================================================================
age
  0_34             10.0535  51.8472 122.2815  12.6207   3.1023   1.0948
  35_51            38.6282  24.4056  29.6252  89.4447  34.5208   3.3755
  52_max           13.4293   6.693    6.3459  50.8984  37.861   81.7724
  [total]          62.1111  82.9457 158.2526 152.9638  75.4841  86.2428
sex
  FEMALE           27.1812  32.2338  77.9304  83.5129  40.3199  44.8218
  MALE             33.9299  49.7119  79.3222  68.4509  34.1642  40.421
  [total]          61.1111  81.9457 157.2526 151.9638  74.4841  85.2428
region
  INNER_CITY       26.1651  46.7431  73.874   60.1973  33.3759  34.6445
  TOWN             24.6991  13.0716  48.4446  53.1731  21.617
17.9946
...
```

The algorithm outputs clusters (columns) and central attribute values in a specific cluster (rows).

How it works...

The necessary clustering classes are located in the `weka.clusters` package. This example demonstrates simple **Expectation Minimization clustering**:

```
import weka.clusterers.EM;
```

Load the data:

```
Instances data = new Instances(new BufferedReader(new
FileReader("dataset/bank-data.arff")));
```

Initialize a clusterer:

```
EM model = new EM();
```

Building a cluster is similar to building a classifier, but instead the `buildClusterer(Instances)` method is called:

```
model.buildClusterer(data);
```

Finally, output the model:

```
System.out.println(model);
EM
==

Number of clusters selected by cross validation: 6

                   Cluster
Attribute            0         1         2         3         4         5
                   (0.1)    (0.13)    (0.26)    (0.25)    (0.12)    (0.14)
=============================================================================
age
  0_34            10.0535   51.8472  122.2815   12.6207    3.1023    1.0948
  35_51           38.6282   24.4056   29.6252   89.4447   34.5208    3.3755
  52_max          13.4293    6.693     6.3459   50.8984   37.861    81.7724
  [total]         62.1111   82.9457  158.2526  152.9638   75.4841   86.2428
  ...
```

The EM created six clusters; the first column lists all the attributes and their average value in a specific cluster is shown in the corresponding column.

There's more...

This section shows additional tasks than can be performed with clustering.

Cluster classification

Clustering can also be used to classify instances similar to classification; the only difference is the method name. So, instead of the `classifyInstance(Instance)` method, call `clusterInstance(Instance)`. You can still use the `distributionForInstance(Instance)` method to obtain the distribution:

```
Instances data = new Instances(new BufferedReader(new
FileReader("dataset/bank-data.arff")));

//load data
Instances data = new Instances(new BufferedReader(new
FileReader("dataset/bank-data.arff")));
```

```
//remove the first instance from dataset
Instance inst = data.instance(0);
data.delete(0);

// new instance of clusterer
EM model = new EM();
// build the clusterer
model.buildClusterer(data);

// classify instance
int cls = model.clusterInstance(inst);
System.out.println("Cluster: "+cls);

double[] dist = model.distributionForInstance(inst);
for(int i = 0; i < dist.length; i++)
    System.out.println("Cluster "+i+".\t"+dist[i]);
```

Here is the output:

```
Cluster: 4
Cluster 0.   0.05197208212603157
Cluster 1.   3.42266240021125E-4
Cluster 2.   2.4532781490129885E-6
Cluster 3.   0.09898134885565614
Cluster 4.   0.8311195273577744
Cluster 5.   0.01753085601118695
Cluster 6.   5.146613118085059E-5
```

The output shows instance distances to each of the clusters.

Incremental clustering

A cluster that implements the weka.clusterers.UpdateableClusterer interface can be trained incrementally similar to classifiers. This is an example using the bank data loaded with weka.core.converters.ArffLoader to train weka.clusterers.Cobweb:

Load the data:

```
// load data
ArffLoader loader = new ArffLoader();
loader.setFile(new File("dataset/bank-data.arff"));
Instances data = loader.getStructure();
```

Call buildClusterer(Instances) with the structure of the dataset (may or may not contain any actual data rows):

```
Cobweb model = new Cobweb();
model.buildClusterer(data);
```

Subsequently, call the `updateClusterer(Instance)` method to feed the clusterer's new `weka.core.Instance` objects, one by one.

```
Instance current;
while ((current = loader.getNextInstance(data)) != null)
    model.updateClusterer(current);
```

Call `updateFinished()` after all `Instance` objects have been processed, for the clusterer to perform additional computations:

```
model.updateFinished();
System.out.println(model);
```

Here is the output:

```
Number of merges: 183
Number of splits: 144
Number of clusters: 850

node 0 [600]
|    node 1 [266]
|    |    node 2 [65]
|    |    |    node 3 [15]
|    |    |    |    node 4 [4]
...
```

The outputted model displays cluster nodes.

Cluster evaluation

A clusterer can be evaluated with the `weka.clusterers.ClusterEvaluation` class.

For example, we can use separate train and test sets, and output the number of clusters found:

```
ClusterEvaluation eval = new ClusterEvaluation();
model.buildClusterer(data);
eval.setClusterer(model);
eval.evaluateClusterer(newData);
System.out.println("# of clusters: " + eval.getNumClusters);
```

Output:

```
# of clusters: 6
```

When density-based clusters are used, cross-validation can be applied as follows (note that the official documentation specifies that with the `MakeDensityBasedClusterer` class, you can turn any clusterer into a density-based one):

```
Instances data = new Instances(new BufferedReader(new
FileReader("dataset/bank-data.arff")));

EM model = new EM();
double logLikelyhood = ClusterEvaluation.crossValidateModel(model,
data, 10, new Random(1));
System.out.println(logLikelyhood);
```

Output:

```
-8.773410259774291
```

The output indicates the log likelihood that cluster distributions in each of the folds match.

Reusing models (Intermediate)

Sometimes, it is useful to build a model and save it for later use. This can be achieved with the `java.io.Serializable` interface that saves an object into a bytestream as a file. The opposite direction, that is, deserialization, restores the bytestream into the original object.

How to do it...

We will first build a sample model, that is, a `J48` decision tree to demonstrate serialization and deserialization:

```
import java.io.BufferedReader;
import java.io.FileReader;

import weka.classifiers.trees.J48;
import weka.core.Instances;
...

J48 cls = new J48();
Instances inst = new Instances(new BufferedReader(new
FileReader("dataset/titanic.arff")));
inst.setClassIndex(inst.numAttributes() - 1);
cls.buildClassifier(inst);

weka.core.SerializationHelper.write("j48.model", cls);

J48 cls2 = (J48) weka.core.SerializationHelper.read("j48.model");
System.out.println(cls2);
```

How it works...

First, we build a sample model, as shown in the *Classification task*.

```
Classifier cls = new J48();

Instances inst = new Instances(new BufferedReader(new FileReader("/
dataset/titanic.arff")));
inst.setClassIndex(inst.numAttributes() - 1);
cls.buildClassifier(inst);
```

Since classifiers have built-in support for serialization, simply call the `write(String, Object)` static method, which is located in the `weka.core.SerializationHelper` package with `String` indicating filename and `Object` as classifier:

```
weka.core.SerializationHelper.write("j48.model", cls);
```

When you need to load the saved classifier, use the `read (String)` method located in the same package. Note, that the `read()` method loads the model as `Object`, so the model needs to be type-casted to an appropriate class, for example, `J48` in our case:

```
J48 cls2 = (J48) weka.core.SerializationHelper.read("j48.model");
```

Classifier is now loaded in the variable named `cls2` and can be used as shown in other recipes.

Data mining in direct marketing (Simple)

In this recipe, we will implement decision making to guide direct marketing in a company. We will use data from a real-world business problem that contains information on customers of an insurance company supplied by the Dutch data-mining company *Sentient Machine Research*. It consists of 86 variables and includes product usage data and socio-demographic data derived from zip area codes. All customers living in areas with the same zip code have the same socio-demographic attributes. The training set contains over 5000 descriptions of customers, while a test set contains 4000 customers. The goal is to predict which of the customers in the train set will buy a caravan insurance policy.

Here is the reference to the TIC Benchmark / CoIL Challenge 2000 data (http://www.liacs.nl/~putten/library/cc2000/):

> P. van der Putten and M. van Someren (eds). CoIL Challenge 2000: The Insurance Company Case. Published by Sentient Machine Research, Amsterdam. Also a Leiden Institute of Advanced Computer Science Technical Report 2000-09. June 22, 2000.

Getting ready

The dataset is available at the UCI Machine Learning Repository (`http://archive.ics.uci.edu/ml/datasets/Insurance+Company+Benchmark+(COIL+2000)`).

The attributes and their values are described in the `TicDataDescr.txt` file. The dataset consists of several separated files with one instance per line with tab delimited fields:

- `TICDATA2000.txt`: Dataset to train and validate prediction models (5822 customer records). Attribute 86, `CARAVAN: Number of mobile home policies`, is the target variable.
- `TICEVAL2000.txt`: Dataset for predictions (4000 customer records). It has the same format as `TICDATA2000.txt`, only the target is missing.
- `TICTGTS2000.txt`: Targets for the evaluation set.

How to do it...

The plan is as follows. First, we will load the `coil-train.arff` dataset into Weka, which was preprocessed from `TICDATA.txt` to start with the recipe immediately.. Then, we will build some prediction models and perform 10-fold-cross validation to obtain preliminary performance. We will select the best one and use it to predict the target value using 10-fold cross-validation. Finally, for the sake of completeness, we will use the best classifier to predict the actual values in the `coil-test.arff` file, although this won't be possible in the real world:

```java
import java.io.BufferedReader;
import java.io.File;
import java.io.FileReader;
import java.util.Random;


import weka.core.converters.ArffLoader;
import weka.classifiers.Classifier;
import weka.classifiers.Evaluation;
import weka.classifiers.bayes.NaiveBayes;
import weka.classifiers.trees.J48;
import weka.core.Instance;
import weka.core.Instances;

public class DirectMarketing {

    public static void main(String args[]) throws Exception {
```

```java
        Instances trainData = new Instances(new BufferedReader(new
FileReader("dataset/coil-train.arff")));

        trainData.setClassIndex(trainData.numAttributes() - 1);

        J48 j48 = new J48();
        j48.setOptions(new String[]{
            "-C", "0.25",   //set confidence factor
            "-M", "2"       //set min num of instances in leaf nodes
        });
        double precision = crossValidation(j48, trainData);
        System.out.println(precision);

        NaiveBayes nb = new NaiveBayes();
        precision = crossValidation(nb, trainData);

        nb.buildClassifier(trainData);

        ArffLoader loader = new ArffLoader();
        loader.setFile(new File("dataset/coil-test.arff"));
        Instances testData = loader.getStructure();
        testData.setClassIndex(trainData.numAttributes() - 1);
        Instance current;
        while ((current = loader.getNextInstance(testData)) != null){
            double cls = nb.classifyInstance(current);
            System.out.println(cls);
        }
    }

    public static double crossValidation(Classifier cls, Instances data)
throws Exception{

        Evaluation eval = new Evaluation(data);
        eval.crossValidateModel(cls, data, 10, new Random(1));
        System.out.println(eval.toSummaryString(false));
        System.out.println(eval.precision(1));
        return eval.precision(1);
    }

}
```

And that's it.

How it works...

Now, let's take a closer look at the code. First, make the following imports:

```java
import java.io.BufferedReader;
import java.io.File;
import java.io.FileReader;
import java.util.Random;

import weka.core.converters.ArffLoader;
import weka.classifiers.Classifier;
import weka.classifiers.Evaluation;
import weka.classifiers.bayes.NaiveBayes;
import weka.classifiers.trees.J48;
import weka.core.Instance;
import weka.core.Instances;

public class DirectMarketing {

  public static void main(String args[]) throws Exception {
```

Next, load the train data:

```java
    Instances trainData = new Instances(new BufferedReader(new FileReader("dataset/coil-train.arff")));

    trainData.setClassIndex(trainData.numAttributes() - 1);
```

Build the decision tree and the Naive Bayes classifier, and evaluate them on the train data with 10-fold-cross validation:

```java
    J48 j48 = new J48();
    j48.setOptions(new String[]{
      "-C", "0.25",    //set confidence factor
      "-M", "2"        //set min num of instances in leaf nodes
    });
    double precision = crossValidation(j48, trainData);
    System.out.println(precision);

    NaiveBayes nb = new NaiveBayes();
    precision = crossValidation(nb, trainData);
```

Naive Bayes achieves better performance, so we will use it to classify real data:

```java
    nb.buildClassifier(trainData);
```

Load the test data:

```
ArffLoader loader = new ArffLoader();
loader.setFile(new File("dataset/coil-test.arff"));
Instances testData = loader.getStructure();
testData.setClassIndex(trainData.numAttributes() - 1);
```

Classify each instance and output results:

```
Instance current;
while ((current = loader.getNextInstance(testData)) != null){
   double cls = nb.classifyInstance(current);
   System.out.println(cls);
}
}
```

The helper method that performs 10-fold-cross validation:

```
public static double crossValidation(Classifier cls, Instances data) 
throws Exception{
```

Initialize new evaluation objects:

```
Evaluation eval = new Evaluation(data);
eval.crossValidateModel(cls, data, 10, new Random(1));
System.out.println(eval.toSummaryString(false));
```

Since the dataset is very unbalanced, use precision for target class `yes` as an evaluation measure:

```
System.out.println(eval.precision(1));
return eval.precision(1);
}

}
```

The output precision shows how accurately the model predicts who will respond to the campaign.

Using Weka for stock value forecasting (Advanced)

The following recipe uses Apple stock data (found in the dataset directory) taken from *Yahoo! finance*. This file contains daily high, low, opening, and closing data for Apple computer stocks from January 3, 2011 to December 31, 2011. Based on the last 12-24 days, we will forecast the next day's closing price.

Getting ready

This recipe requires Weka developer version and forecasting module (introduced in versions greater than Weka 3.7.3) named `timeseriesForecasting1.0.10.zip`, which can be downloaded from `http://sourceforge.net/projects/weka/files/weka-packages/`.

Add the following JAR to the class path of your local machine:

`-classpath ".;C:\Program Files (x86)\Weka-3-7\weka.jar;C:\Weka-3-7\timeseriesForecasting\pdm-timeseriesforecasting-ce-TRUNK-SNAPSHOT.jar"`

How to do it...

Follow this snippet:

```java
import java.io.*;

import java.util.List;
import weka.core.Instances;
import weka.classifiers.functions.GaussianProcesses;
import weka.classifiers.evaluation.NumericPrediction;
import weka.classifiers.timeseries.WekaForecaster;

public class TimeSeriesExample {

  public static void main(String[] args) {
    try {

      Instances dataset = new Instances(new BufferedReader(new FileReader("dataset/appl.arff")));
      dataset.sort(0);

      WekaForecaster forecaster = new WekaForecaster();
      forecaster.setFieldsToForecast("Close");

      forecaster.setBaseForecaster(new GaussianProcesses());

      forecaster.getTSLagMaker().setTimeStampField("Date");
      forecaster.getTSLagMaker().setMinLag(12);
      forecaster.getTSLagMaker().setMaxLag(24);

      forecaster.buildForecaster(dataset);
```

```
            forecaster.primeForecaster(dataset);

            List<NumericPrediction> predsAtStep = forecast.get(i);
            NumericPrediction predForTarget = predsAtStep.get(0);
            System.out.println("" + predForTarget.predicted() + " ");

      } catch (Exception ex) {
        ex.printStackTrace();
      }
    }
  }
}
```

This code snippet outputs the next stock value.

How it works...

First, make the following imports.

```
import java.io.*;

import java.util.List;
import weka.core.Instances;
import weka.classifiers.functions.GaussianProcesses;
import weka.classifiers.evaluation.NumericPrediction;
import weka.classifiers.timeseries.WekaForecaster;

public class TimeSeriesExample {

  public static void main(String[] args) {
    try {
```

Load the stock data:

```
      Instances dataset = new Instances(new BufferedReader(new
FileReader("dataset/appl.arff")));
```

Sort the data by date (that is, the first attribute):

```
      dataset.sort(0);
```

Initialize a new forecaster:

```
      WekaForecaster forecaster = new WekaForecaster();
```

Set the target variables we want to forecast:

```
      forecaster.setFieldsToForecast("Close");
```

Replace the `SMOreg` default classifier with Gaussian processes:

```
forecaster.setBaseForecaster(new GaussianProcesses());
```

Specify that the `Date` attribute contains the timestamp field:

```
forecaster.getTSLagMaker().setTimeStampField("Date");
```

The forecaster constructs a window of samples over a time period to allow the forecasting algorithm to capture the relationship between past and current value. The minimum and maximum lags define the number of past steps to be included in the window:

```
forecaster.getTSLagMaker().setMinLag(12);
forecaster.getTSLagMaker().setMaxLag(24);
```

Build the forecaster:

```
forecaster.buildForecaster(dataset);
```

Put enough recent historical data to cover the maximum lag. In our case, we just specify the complete dataset:

```
forecaster.primeForecaster(dataset);
```

Forecast the next value and output predictions:

```
      List<NumericPrediction> predsAtStep = forecast.get(0);
      NumericPrediction predForTarget = predsAtStep.get(0);
      System.out.println("" + predForTarget.predicted() + " ");

    } catch (Exception ex) {
      ex.printStackTrace();
    }
  }
}
```

The outputted number is the next predicted value. You can then use this value in your decision logic, for example, if the predicted value is higher than the current value, then generate buy signal

Recommendation system (Advanced)

In this recipe, we will implement a recommendation system. Typically, there are two ways to provide recommendations: items frequently bought together, and customers who bought this item also bought... The first problem can be solved with association rules, as shown in the *Association rules* recipe. The second question is trickier, and this recipe will show you how to address it with a technique called **collaborative filtering**.

Our task will be to implement a movie recommendation system. The dataset consists of user ratings on scale 1-10 for the first 87 movies in the IMDB Top 250 List. If a user provides a rating for a couple of movies, the system can say: "Users who liked these movies, also liked...".

> The presented approach is inspired by Marina Barsky's lecture materials (http://csci.viu.ca/~barskym/).

Getting ready

The dataset is available in the source code bundle. The first file, `movieRatings.arff`, contains user ratings for each movie on the scale of 1-10. Each attribute corresponds to a movie, while each data line corresponds to user ratings. If a user rating is missing, then the rating is 0.

The second file, `user.arff`, has the same attribute structure, but a single data line that corresponds to ratings of the current user. Our task is to provide recommendations to this user.

How to do it...

The plan is as follows. First, we will load the `movieRatings.arff` and `user.arff` datasets into Weka. Then, we will find five users in `movieRatings.arff` that have a similar taste as our current user in `user.arff`. Finally, we will rank the movies, which have not yet been rated by the current user:

```
import weka.core.*;
import weka.core.converters.ConverterUtils.DataSource;
import weka.core.neighboursearch.LinearNNSearch;
import java.io.*;

import java.util.*;
public class Recommender {
  public static void main(String[] args) throws Exception {

    DataSource source = new DataSource("dataset/movieRatings.arff");
    Instances dataset = source.getDataSet();

    source = new DataSource("dataset/user.arff");
    Instances userRating = source.getDataSet();
    Instance userData = userRating.firstInstance();

    LinearNNSearch kNN = new LinearNNSearch(dataset);
```

```java
    Instances neighbors = null;
    double[] distances = null;

    try {
      neighbors = kNN.kNearestNeighbours(userData, 5);
      distances = kNN.getDistances();
    } catch (Exception e) {
      System.out.println("Neighbors could not be found.");
      return;
    }

    double[] similarities = new double[distances.length];
    for (int i = 0; i < distances.length; i++) {
      similarities[i] = 1.0 / distances[i];
    }

    Enumeration nInstances = neighbors.enumerateInstances();

    Map<String, List<Integer>> recommendations = new HashMap<String,
List<Integer>>();
    for(int i = 0; i < neighbors.numInstances(); i++){
      Instance currNeighbor = neighbors.get(i);

        for (int j = 0; j < currNeighbor.numAttributes(); j++) {
          if (userData.value(j) < 1) {
            String attrName = userData.attribute(j).name();
            List<Integer> lst = new ArrayList<Integer>();
            if (recommendations.containsKey(attrName)) {
              lst = recommendations.get(attrName);
            }

            lst.add((int)currNeighbor.value(j));
            recommendations.put(attrName, lst);
          }
        }

    }

    List<RecommendationRecord> finalRanks = new ArrayList<Recommendat
ionRecord>();

    Iterator<String> it = recommendations.keySet().iterator();
    while (it.hasNext()) {
      String atrName = it.next();
```

```java
      double totalImpact = 0;
      double weightedSum = 0;
      List<Integer> ranks = recommendations.get(atrName);
      for (int i = 0; i < ranks.size(); i++) {
        int val = ranks.get(i);
        totalImpact += similarities[i];
        weightedSum += (double) similarities[i] * val;
      }
      RecommendationRecord rec = new RecommendationRecord();
      rec.attributeName = atrName;
      rec.score = weightedSum / totalImpact;

      finalRanks.add(rec);
    }
    Collections.sort(finalRanks);

    // print top 3 recommendations
    System.out.println(finalRanks.get(0));
    System.out.println(finalRanks.get(1));
    System.out.println(finalRanks.get(2));
  }
```

The outputs are the top three movie recommendations:

```
The Great Dictator (1940): 1.8935866254179377
The Lord of the Rings: The Fellowship of the Ring (2001):
1.7664942763356077
Schindler s List (1993): 1.5456824917936567
```

The recommendations (and their score) can be now displayed to the user.

How it works...

First, make the following imports:

```java
import weka.core.*;
import weka.core.converters.ConverterUtils.DataSource;
import weka.core.neighboursearch.LinearNNSearch;
import java.io.*;
import java.util.*;
```

Note, that we have imported `weka.core.neighboursearch.LinearNNSearch`, it will help us to find users with similar tastes.

Start a new class and import the movie ratings dataset, as well as ratings of our current user:

```
public class Recommender {
  public static void main(String[] args) throws Exception {

    // read learning dataset
    DataSource source = new DataSource("dataset/movieRatings.arff");
    Instances dataset = source.getDataSet();

    // read user data
    source = new DataSource("dataset/user.arff");
    Instances userRating = source.getDataSet();
    Instance userData = userRating.firstInstance();
```

Initialize a nearest-neighbor search. This is a brute force search algorithm that finds the nearest neighbors of the given instance. It is initialized with the movie ratings dataset:

```
    LinearNNSearch kNN = new LinearNNSearch(dataset);
    Instances neighbors = null;
    double[] distances = null;

    try {
```

Call the `kNN.kNearestNeighbours (Instance, int)` method to perform a nearest-neighbor search. We pass our current user `userData` instance, and specify to find five nearest neighbors:

```
      neighbors = kNN.kNearestNeighbours(userData, 5);
```

Call `kNN.getDistances()` to obtain the `double[]` table that specifies how far away the neighbors are:

```
      distances = kNN.getDistances();
    } catch (Exception e) {
      System.out.println("Neighbors could not be found.");
      return;
    }
```

We define similarity between users as 1/distance; that is, the bigger the distance, the smaller the similarity. We will use similarities to weigh how much should neighbor preferences contribute to the overall movie rating:

```
    double[] similarities = new double[distances.length];
    for (int i = 0; i < distances.length; i++) {
      similarities[i] = 1.0 / distances[i];
      //System.out.println(similarities[i]);
    }
```

Ok, now we are ready to rank the movies. We will have a double loop. The first loop will go over each neighbor, while the second loop will go over each movie. If the current user has not rated the movie, we will collect the rating provided by the neighbor and store it in `HashMap<String, List<Integer>>()`. `HashMap` consists of a `String` key that corresponds to a movie title, and a list of integers that contain ratings for each of the neighbors:

```
Enumeration nInstances = neighbors.enumerateInstances();
Map<String, List<Integer>> recommendations = new HashMap<String,
List<Integer>>();
```

The first loop over each neighbor:

```
for(int i = 0; i < neighbors.numInstances(); i++){
    Instance currNeighbor = neighbors.get(i);
```

The second loop over each movie:

```
for (int j = 0; j < currNeighbor.numAttributes(); j++) {
```

If the movie is not ranked by the current user:

```
if (userData.value(j) < 1) {
```

Retrieve the name of the movie:

```
String attrName = userData.attribute(j).name();
```

Initialize a new integer list (if this is the first neighbor) or use an existing one:

```
List<Integer> lst = new ArrayList<Integer>();
if (recommendations.containsKey(attrName)) {
   lst = recommendations.get(attrName);
}
```

Append the neighbor's rating to the list of ratings for the current movie:

```
lst.add((int)currNeighbor.value(j));
```

Save the ratings in the hashmap:

```
        recommendations.put(attrName, lst);
      }
    }
  }
}
```

Ok, so now we have collected the neighbors' ratings for each of the movies. The next task to compute the move is the final recommendation score. We will simply summarize the neighbors' ratings and weigh them by similarity; more similar neighbors will contribute more to the overall recommendation score.

We create a new list of the `RecommendationRecord` objects (implemented in the source code bundle), which can store movie titles and scores:

```
List<RecommendationRecord> finalRanks = new ArrayList<Recommendat
ionRecord>();
```

Now, we loop over hashmap items – movies:

```
Iterator<String> it = recommendations.keySet().iterator();
while (it.hasNext()) {
  String atrName = it.next();
  double totalImpact = 0;
  double weightedSum = 0;
```

And loop over neighbors' recommendations:

```
List<Integer> ranks = recommendations.get(atrName);
for (int i = 0; i < ranks.size(); i++) {
```

Get a neighbor's ranking:

```
  int val = ranks.get(i);
```

Accumulate similarity weight:

```
  totalImpact += similarities[i];
```

Accumulate recommendation score:

```
  weightedSum += (double) similarities[i] * val;
}
```

Create a new `RecommendationRecord` object, store the movie title and normalized score:

```
RecommendationRecord rec = new RecommendationRecord();
rec.attributeName = atrName;
rec.score = weightedSum / totalImpact;

finalRanks.add(rec);
}
```

After all the recommendation scores are computed, sort the collection of `RecommendationRecord` objects (`RecommendationRecord` implements a comparable interface):

```
Collections.sort(finalRanks);
```

Finally, print the top three recommendations with their scores:

```
    // print top 3 recommendations
    System.out.println(finalRanks.get(0));
    System.out.println(finalRanks.get(1));
    System.out.println(finalRanks.get(2));
}
```

That's it. The preceding recipe can be easily modified to recommend other items such as music, books, grocery items, and so on.

**Thank you for buying
Instant Weka How-to**

About Packt Publishing

Packt, pronounced 'packed', published its first book "*Mastering phpMyAdmin for Effective MySQL Management*" in April 2004 and subsequently continued to specialize in publishing highly focused books on specific technologies and solutions.

Our books and publications share the experiences of your fellow IT professionals in adapting and customizing today's systems, applications, and frameworks. Our solution based books give you the knowledge and power to customize the software and technologies you're using to get the job done. Packt books are more specific and less general than the IT books you have seen in the past. Our unique business model allows us to bring you more focused information, giving you more of what you need to know, and less of what you don't.

Packt is a modern, yet unique publishing company, which focuses on producing quality, cutting-edge books for communities of developers, administrators, and newbies alike. For more information, please visit our website: www.packtpub.com.

Writing for Packt

We welcome all inquiries from people who are interested in authoring. Book proposals should be sent to author@packtpub.com. If your book idea is still at an early stage and you would like to discuss it first before writing a formal book proposal, contact us; one of our commissioning editors will get in touch with you.

We're not just looking for published authors; if you have strong technical skills but no writing experience, our experienced editors can help you develop a writing career, or simply get some additional reward for your expertise.

[PACKT] PUBLISHING

Java 7 JAX-WS Web Services

ISBN: 978-1-84968-720-1 Paperback: 64 pages

A practical, focused mini book for creating Web Services in Java 7

1. Develop Java 7 JAX-WS web services using the NetBeans IDE and Oracle GlassFish server
2. End-to-end application which makes use of the new clientjar option in JAX-WS wsimport tool
3. Packed with ample screenshots and practical instructions

Java 7 New Features Cookbook

ISBN: 978-1-84968-562-7 Paperback: 384 pages

Over 100 comprehensive recipes to get you up to speed with all the exciting new features of Java 7

1. Comprehensive coverage of the new features of Java 7 organized around easy-to-follow recipes
2. Covers exciting features such as the try-with-resources block, the monitoring of directory events, asynchronous IO and new GUI enhancements, and more
3. A learn-by-example based approach that focuses on key concepts to provide the foundation to solve real world problems

Please check **www.PacktPub.com** for information on our titles

Building Machine Learning Systems with Python

ISBN: 978-1-78216-140-0　　　Paperback: 350 pages

Master the art of Python Machine Learning and successfully implement it in your projects and build effective ML systems

1. A practical, scenario-based tutorial to get into the right mind set of a machine learner (data exploration)
2. Master the diverse ML Python libraries and start building your Python-based ML systems
3. Wide and practical coverage of ML areas to immediately implement in your projects - Regression, Recommender Systems, Computer Vision, and much more

Java EE 6 with GlassFish 3 Application Server

ISBN: 978-1-84951-036-3　　　Paperback: 488 pages

A practical guide to install and configure the GlassFish 3 Application Server and Develop Java EE 6 applications to be deployed to this server

1. Install and configure the GlassFish 3 Application Server and develop Java EE 6 applications to be deployed to this server
2. Specialize in all major Java EE 6 APIs, including new additions to the specification such as CDI and JAX-RS
3. Use GlassFish v3 application server and gain enterprise reliability and performance with less complexity

Please check www.PacktPub.com for information on our titles

Printed in Great Britain
by Amazon